THROUGH OUR EYES

WHAT A RIDE

Copyright © 2019 by Bill Hayden

All rights reserved

Hayden, Bill
Through Our Eyes, What A Ride: A Father's Stories About Raising Athletes
ISBN 978-0-578-57574-2

1. Biography & Autobiography / Personal Memoirs. 2. Sports & Recreation / Football. 3. Sports & Recreation / Coaching. 4. Family & Relationships / Fatherhood.

For more information, contact the author at billmhayden@aol.com

Printed in the U.S.A.
Distributed by Ingram

THROUGH OUR EYES

WHAT A RIDE

A FATHER'S STORIES
ABOUT RAISING ATHLETES

BILL HAYDEN

	Introduction	
1	Football as a Youth	1
2	Football in High School	6
3	The Awards and Recognition	19
4	Playing Football in College	26
5	Senior Year in College	48
6	Nick's First NFL Team, The Carolina Panthers	64
7	The Cincinnati Bengals Come Calling	84
8	The Dallas Cowboys	90
9	Another NFL Team, or Time to Retire?	107
10	Life After Football	112
	The Ride Never Ends	117

Introduction

It's every boy's dream to someday play football in the NFL, and I was no exception. I was blessed to be able to play through college at the University of Wisconsin-Whitewater as an offensive tackle. I'd wanted to continue to play football after college and had an opportunity to play semi-pro ball for the Racine Gladiators. A teammate who graduated a year before me was playing for the Gladiators, and he mentioned that an offensive guard was retiring, and so there was an opening. Unfortunately, three days after graduating from college, I was in a motorcycle accident, and suddenly my football career was over. It was devastating to me because, in my mind, I was not done playing football. I still remember my last game in college, and how much I was still learning and growing, and I was excited for the next step.

Life is funny and sometimes we never know the whys. However, now I can honestly say that if I'd had a choice to play in the NFL or have a son play in the NFL, I would have chosen having a son play, because it actually happened and has been so special. I always wanted my boys to play football and experience what I had. I was so blessed to have had so many great coaches who not only taught me the game of football but also taught me so much about life. One of the biggest mentors in my life was a high school coach who took the time out of his busy schedule to help me become a better football player, both on and off the field, and more important, a better person in this world. I still teach every day the principles I learned from him. I call this my "give-back" to others for what I have been so fortunate to receive in my life.

This book is dedicated to my wife, Mary, who has put up with me for thirty-five years and has been instrumental in what we have achieved with our children and with sports. Mary and I went to high school together in Muskego, Wisconsin. She is the true athlete in our family, excelling in every sport she's played, and to this day she is very good in whatever sport she plays. I was big and strong but did not have the athletic ability to play beyond college, but I gave it all I had and enjoyed every minute of my football career. I have memories now of my experiences, and I do cherish them, and I am always excited to watch a Whitewater football game. Now simply spectators, my wife and I have experienced something not many parents get to, and that is having a son who excelled in football, not only in high school and college but also in the NFL.

This book is about the stories and memories Mary and I went through at each stage of our children's time in sports. In the end, I can truly say: "What a ride!" It's an honor to be able to write about a parent's perspective of having children who played sports, and, of course, having a son who played football in the NFL.

I hope all who read this book enjoy it as much as I did writing all the stories and memories, because as you will see, so many people in our lives have enjoyed the experience as much as we have. As you read the stories, you will learn that there is much more than just a talented football player playing in the NFL. It's about what it takes to be great in life at all levels, such as being on time, developing a work ethic, making an effort, having the right attitude, living with passion, doing the extras, and being coachable and prepared. These are all positive attributes that make you successful both on and off the field, no matter what sport you play.

CHAPTER 1

FOOTBALL AS A YOUTH

I started playing football when I was in eighth grade, and as time goes on (as with anything), the next generation starts to do things even earlier. This was no exception for my first son, who started playing tackle football in sixth grade. I still can remember the beginning. We were so excited that our son was going to play football. This was new to us because now we were becoming spectators and not playing the sports ourselves.

I still remember my son getting his football equipment and seeing the excitement in his eyes as he wore his football uniform, prancing around the house before the first day of practice. I remember watching my son practice for the first time and realizing how much he was going to have to learn. It was evident that I did not have a superstar in the beginning. Actually, it was very hard to watch because my son was falling over his own two feet. I remember saying to myself at one point, *I'm glad I have a healthy boy because it does not appear he's going to do very well in football.*

As with most boys at that age, the coaches have them try many different positions. Nick was not huge, but he was big enough that they played him on both the offensive and defensive side of the ball. Nick became a fullback but did not play that much at that position in the beginning. Nick was moved to a linebacker, and he eventually became the starter. As time went

WHAT A RIDE

on that first year, we began to see some improvement. I do know he was enjoying himself and looked forward to playing in the games and practicing each day, which is half the battle.

My wife and I really enjoyed watching him improve throughout the year and started to realize that we were hanging out with the other "football parents," who became our new friends. To this day, my wife and I have met some great parents, many of whom we have maintained friendships with throughout the years. No matter what sport your child plays, it is the friends you make from being involved with these activities that is so memorable, and it is through the commonality of sports that truly creates this experience.

Nick continued to play in seventh grade and was growing and improving each year. He did win the position of fullback that year and was also the starting linebacker. As a matter of fact, in seventh grade Nick did receive an award. Not for being the best athlete or for running for 100 yards but for being the most improved football player on the team that year. It was the start of something big.

Nick also began to learn what it was like to be on a winning team. The team did very well every year, with a winning record. In eighth grade Nick grew too much and had to play center because there were weight restrictions for fullback and linebacker. I do remember in eighth grade I began to work out Nick in the off-season. I came up with a training program that I'd remembered from when I was in college, and I taught Nick what to do to condition himself in the off-season. I remember taking Nick through the exercises and routines, and I loved working him out. One of the early signs I recognized was that Nick was self-motivated. I did not have to hound him to work out. Once he got the workout down, he practiced in the yard every day, and I would just ask when I came home from work if he had done the workout, and he always said yes. To me, to be a great athlete, the first thing is: you must be self-motivated and must enjoy it every day. I did see that with Nick and with my son Alex and daughter Abbey.

Football as a Youth

I also remember buying Nick new Strength Shoes in eighth grade. The shoes had a big circle platform on the bottom of the shoe at the front and were meant to build up your calves as you worked out. I know Nick used them for a while, but they were not the trick that made him a superstar. I know Nick did not like the shoes, and they finally sat on a shelf, collecting dust. I also remember Nick going through growth spurts, his heels and knees hurting him very bad, to the point he would cry at night. We took him to the doctor and learned that he did not have any knee or heel problems, but because his body was growing faster than his tendons, they were stretching and causing the pain. It was very hard watching my child go through pain and not being able to help him. The doctor said he would have to play through it or stop playing football. The only remedy he gave us was to roll a can of beans under his foot to relieve some of the pain. Nick played through the pain, and it actually continued into his high school years.

Nick had a second love, and it was basketball. Nick went to a parochial grade school called St. Luke's, and the school was big on basketball. Nick began to excel more in basketball than football, and in eighth grade the team took the Padre Sera tournament, which is like winning a state championship in high school. There is no doubt that his playing basketball helped him develop into a better football player and truly complemented his workouts for football.

When Nick was in eighth grade, we had to start making some choices. Most kids from his parochial school went on to a Catholic high school. Mary and I did not think we could afford paying for both high school and then college and decided that paying for our children's college was more important (which we did for all of our children) and decided that we would send our kids to public high school. We also wanted to move farther out in the country and found a house in North Lake, Wisconsin, that we really liked. Like most parents, this was a very hard decision, but a decision that truly influenced all of our kids positively, including Nick, with playing both football and

What a Ride

basketball in high school. North Lake was in the Arrowhead School District, and we had heard that Arrowhead was a great academic school, which was very important to us; but as we learned, they also were great in football. I had never met the high school football coach, but to our surprise he had heard of Nick Hayden. Within our first week of moving to North Lake, we received a wonderful handwritten card from the coach welcoming us to the community and talking about what a great choice we'd made by sending Nick to Arrowhead, not only for the academics, but also because of his future as a football player. As naive parents at that time, it never dawned on us that coaches were watching him grow. The first time we met with his coach, he said he knew Nick was going to be special, and he started out by saying that he knew Nick was going to be big in size because both Mary and I were bigger in size. It was amazing how much he knew about us, and we did not really know him at all. The next thing that came out of his new coach's mouth was that he'd started his football career at Franklin High School. Both my wife and I went to Muskego High School, which was in the same conference as Franklin. Coach went on to say that he remembered Muskego football being rated first in state. At that time (twenty years ago), Franklin was not having a good year; they'd played us in Muskego, and we were undefeated. Franklin beat us that day, and it took us out of the rankings. Coach said he knew everything about me back in high school, and they ran their offense at me that day, making sure I was double teamed on every play. It was amazing to listen to him because he did remember so many details from twenty years ago, and I never realized I'd made such an impact on a coach I didn't even know.

Then the second story he told really got to me. He told Nick he remembered when I was in high school wrestling; he saw me pin my opponent in seven seconds, and I took the guy with one arm and flipped him onto his back. His coach told him that he had never seen someone do that before. I loved the stories, and it was the start of a great relationship with my son's coach.

Football as a Youth

Ironically, the coach had told those and other stories many times throughout Nick's career. It has always been a highlight of mine to hear those stories and know that my son was playing for a coach who saw me play football when I was in high school.

The most ironic thing is to this day is that most people think we moved to North Lake so our son could play on a great football team, but the truth is we had just found a house out in the country that we fell in love with. It truly had nothing to do with football, but now looking back on it, it was probably the best decision Mary and I ever made for all of our children, both academically and for sports.

CHAPTER 2

Football in High School

As a freshman, Nick played on the football team as a linebacker. There were no weight restrictions, so he could play any position. Nick began to really grow into his body, and it started becoming evident he was going to be one of the tallest and biggest players on the team. As we went through the season, we began to see Nick excel in football. He became a lot faster and a lot stronger. We could see his technique begin to improve, and there was no doubt he understood the game of football. Right from the beginning, Nick began telling his teammates what gap to be in, or what to do on certain plays. I prided myself with understanding the game of football, and it was great to see my son doing the same things I had done—helping teammates with plays and being a motivator to them. As much as we saw improvement in our son, it never dawned on us at that time there would be so many things to come that were so special. My wife and I were enjoying watching him play and meeting so many great parents who have been great friends for so many years now.

My younger son, Alex, was now starting his football career on the peewee league. I was now doing the same things with Alex as I had done with Nick. It was so exciting to me having both of my sons playing football. Right from the beginning Alex decided he wanted to be an offensive tackle, like I was in

Football in High School

high school and college. There is nothing better than knowing my son wants to play the same position as I did, and it does make it a lot easier to train and teach the position I had played. I also remember working out Alex in the summers. The funny thing is you even start earlier with the training program with your second child than the first. Alex was growing and getting better with each game he played in. We were blessed again with the coaching staff, and we were meeting parents from his grade and enjoying going to every game.

As a sophomore Nick did start on varsity and split reps as a tight end on offense with a more seasoned player. The team was ranked first in state that year and had a great season but did lose in the first game of the playoffs. You could now see that Nick had some potential to be a very good football player, and at the end of the season, we saw a lot of improvement in him. As we learned later from his coach, there were so many great athletes on the team, it was hard to find a spot for Nick on the team and that is why he split time with a teammate as a tight end, because that was where the need was.

After Nick's sophomore year in football amazing things started to happen. We received word that Nick had received a scholarship offer from Nebraska. As many people know, college football in Nebraska is very big, and we could not believe our son was starting to receive scholarship offers. My wife and I could not believe that college recruiters were noticing our son at such a young age. This was all new to us and it was very humbling to know that we had a son who may play football for a Division 1 school someday. Nick's coach began to receive more and more scholarships from colleges but was very good at making sure we just sat back and waited until the right time to start looking at them.

Nick's junior year he started both ways, as a tight end and defensive end. The team again was rated in state. This year the team went on through the playoffs and made it to the state game. For those who do not know this, the game is played at Camp Randall Stadium in Madison, Wisconsin, which is an honor for

WHAT A RIDE

Nick, #5, walking to the Arrowhead field with teammates before a game

any child to play in. I still remember the day and getting up early to see the players off in the bus at their school. It was amazing to see so many people from the community supporting them as they left Hartland to go to Madison.

All the parents' cars were all painted up with Arrowhead colors and players' numbers. We had many family and friends who went up to Madison with us. We left right after the team did on the bus and spent the day in Madison before the game that started at 4 p.m. Once we got into the stadium, it was so surreal. It was hard to believe our son was playing in this beautiful stadium for a high school state championship. The game started, and on the third play of the game an offensive tackle from the opposing team blocked low on Nick and injured his ankle. This is one of the hardest things to see. We knew immediately he was injured, but he did not come out of the game. It was so hard to watch each play because Nick was literally playing on one leg and still making plays. My wife was devastated. This was her son, and her motherly instincts kicked in. At halftime, with a tied game, Mary suddenly looked at me and said, "I need to go see if Nick is okay."

Football in High School

I blurted out, "You cannot do that!" But Mary was already halfway down the bleachers, heading to the locker room. I remember seeing a security guard by the entrance and somehow she passed him to go toward the locker rooms underneath the stadium. Mary returned before halftime was over, and I asked if she was able to see Nick. Mary said no, but she'd tried her hardest to find him.

What we learned after the game from the players and Nick is that Mary did get to the door of the locker room, and the door was locked, and she was pounding on the door shouting that she wanted to see Nick to see how he was doing. They did not let Mary in, which is no surprise, but they knew it was Nick's mom, and it has been a great story ever since. Mary did wait for them to come out of the tunnel, though, and was screaming at the players to fight to the end and go out and win. Still to this day, when we see some of Nick's teammates from high school, that story always comes up, and everyone always says only Nick's mom could do something like that.

Unfortunately, the team lost the game by a late fourth-quarter touchdown, and it really does take all the wind out of you, not only as a football player but as a parent, too. It was a sad drive home, but once we got back to the high school and greeted all the players, it was such a fantastic experience that it did not matter anymore. We all had so much fun, and we realized that we still had another year to play football and try to win a state championship. For Nick, he had to wait for about a month to play basketball because he had received a high ankle sprain that took a while to heal.

After the season, we received such a big surprise. Nick had made all-state as a defensive lineman and was the defensive player of the year. We knew Nick had a great season, but we also knew that there are so many great football players in the state that it truly was a surprise that our son received such a high honor. We had known this was a possibility because my brother-in-law was coaching high school football at the time and told us he had some inside information, specifically that

WHAT A RIDE

Nick was going to be an all-state defensive lineman. But until we were informed, we were not sure whether this was true.

In addition, the scholarships continued to come in. We never saw every scholarship but did hear from his coach he received over fifty scholarships from Division 1 football programs. We discussed what the top scholarships were and Nick decided the top three he would like to pursue were Michigan, Wisconsin, and Notre Dame in that order.

You may wonder why Michigan was his top school and not the Wisconsin Badgers, since he grew up in Wisconsin. I can tell you why. As a kid, Nick loved to watch Michigan football. Michigan was such an elite program at the time, and Nick was a young football player saying he would love to play for Michigan someday. Now he had an opportunity to do just that because he was offered a scholarship. Mary and I were so excited. One thing we began to learn very quickly was that we could help guide Nick and talk things through with him, but Mary and I agreed that no matter what we thought, it had to be up to Nick in the end.

You will see this throughout the book. We stuck to that philosophy, and I would recommend to any parent in the same situation to do just that, because the child earned it and it has to be what they want, not what the parents want. One of the things his coach had recommended is that we visit early and that Nick should try to make a decision on the school before his senior year. Part of this was just in case he got injured his senior year while playing football, the chances would be slim the school would retract the scholarship; and the other part was it would take the load off Nick's shoulders knowing where he was going and he could truly enjoy his senior year in high school playing football.

Nick's coach was so knowledgeable about the process and kept us informed but never once tried to persuade Nick or us to go in any particular direction. The trust and respect we had for his coach was huge to us as a family.

The coaches from Michigan began talking to Nick and informing him of everything he needed to know. There are

Football in High School

times when the coaches can talk to your son, and there are dead periods (set by the rules) when they cannot talk to you. We learned early on to make sure to follow every rule so that we did not jeopardize the scholarship. I am sure those reading this book have read about the consequences when the rules are broken. We took this very seriously and never broke a rule or jeopardized our son in any way, and no coach that we talked to or met with ever did this, either.

The time came for Nick to make his official visit with Michigan. We were so excited to go to Michigan; we packed up the entire family and headed to Michigan for his first visit. This was at least a five-hour drive, so we made sure to add an hour to the trip so we were not late. We were driving along, and for those who may not know, Michigan is in a different time zone and is one hour ahead of Wisconsin. Well, we realized that during the trip to Michigan, which now added a little stress to the drive. *Are we going to make it in time?* Well, we decided to call the coach on the way and let him know we could be a little late because we'd forgotten about the change in time zones, and the coach said there was no issue. We also did not know what to expect or what would happen that day, so there were many unknowns.

We did arrive fifteen minutes late and walked into the front door of the football office. The first thing we saw was fifty to sixty other football recruits waiting in the lobby. What a sight, and the first thing we thought about was: *Wow, our son is going to have to compete with all these players for a scholarship.*

All of a sudden, someone in the crowd said, "The Haydens are here," and out came the head coach of Michigan, walked right over to us, and introduced himself right in front of all these other football recruits. The head football coach said to us (the entire family), "Come with me."

We left the other football recruits and began the tour, with him being our escort. The coach was such a gentleman from the beginning. He explained everything in such detail. He acted as if Nick was already on the team. The coach took us through the

WHAT A RIDE

entire facility showing us things, like the weight room, the locker room, the All-American room, the place where the athletes eat every day and the study area. Then to our surprise, the head coach took us to his office. It was absolutely breathtaking. One wall was all windows that overlooked the football stadium. It was beautiful. His office was so unbelievable, with so many trophies and pictures and a huge desk and a nice sitting area.

"Please sit down," he said. Now in this sitting area was a beautiful leather couch. The coach looked at me and said, "Bill, come sit with me on the couch." I did. The coach then began asking all of us questions. He was so smooth and very much a gentleman. He asked questions of my kids and they answered; he asked several questions of my wife and she answered. One thing I am very blessed with is that my wife is so personable that she always makes a great impression with everyone, and this day was no exception. Mary is definitely my better half.

Then he began asking Nick many questions about football and why he wanted to play for Michigan. Nick was very direct and answered all his questions. I was very proud of him the way he presented himself. Then it was my turn. The coach started asking me questions about my football career, my work career, how long we were married and so on. You have to remember I was sitting right next to him on the beautiful leather couch and I was in awe. He had just learned so much about my entire family and never once talked about himself. He was a true gentleman and someone I now realized would be a great head coach to my son. He leaned over to me, put his arm around my neck, looked straight in my eyes, and said, "Nick's coming to Michigan, right!"

I was flabbergasted and just recall saying, "Yeahhh."

He said, "Well, we are looking forward to him being a Wolverine."

We then left the head coach, met with several other coaches that day, and got a tour of the entire campus. On the way home we were all so excited, especially Nick, because he was going to play for the team he so much admired as a child. To me it was a dream come true.

Football in High School

Nick was so excited and continued to stay in contact with the coaches at Michigan. We were excited because we were going to be able to watch our son play football after high school. Everything seemed to be set with Michigan, but about four months later Nick came home and said he was going to go to Madison for about three days to check out the campus. Nick said that his high school quarterback who had graduated the year before got a scholarship to Wisconsin to play football and invited him up to see the campus. We knew the family very well and thought it would be good for Nick to confirm that Michigan was the place he wanted to play football.

Nick went up to Madison for those three days, and we really did not hear from him. When he came home and walked through the door, I asked Nick how his visit to Madison went. The first words out of his mouth were, "I am going to Wisconsin to play football."

Both Mary and I looked at him and said, "What? All your life you've wanted to play football for Michigan and you loved the first visit, and now you want to play football at Wisconsin!" We asked Nick, why the change? All Nick said was, "I think it is the right place for me to play football in college, and I now want to play football for the Wisconsin Badgers."

We told Nick that if this was the case, then maybe we should also go to Notre Dame and visit that school to see if he liked that school. Nick was very straightforward and said, "I do not want to go to Notre Dame or Michigan anymore; I want to play football at Wisconsin."

Mary and I said, "OK, Nick, let's give it a week or so and see if this is truly what you want or if we should continue to look and visit other colleges." A week went by and again Mary and I asked Nick if he still wanted to play football for the Wisconsin Badgers or continue with Michigan or visit other colleges. Nick said that his mind was made up and he wanted to play football for the Wisconsin Badgers. We then told Nick he would have to inform his high school coach of his change of heart. Nick did just that and his coach then contacted the head coach at Wisconsin and informed him of the change.

WHAT A RIDE

The next thing we found out was that the head coach from Wisconsin and some of his assistants wanted to come to our home and visit with us. We set up a date and time and did have them to our house. I still remember the evening. We had a fire in the fireplace in our family room; my wife had made some special hors d'oeuvres for the coaches, and we really wanted to make it special for Nick that night. The coaches came in and we proceeded to the family room. The coaches began to sit down. I had a leather couch in my family room, and the head coach sat down on the couch. Like the coach from Michigan, he looked at me and said to sit next to him on the couch. The only difference was this was *my* leather couch this time. We began talking, and the head coach asked all of us many questions about our lives. The coach then began asking questions of Nick and why he wanted to be a Badger. Nick proceeded to tell him and he also answered any questions Nick or we had. Then, as I had experienced with the Michigan head coach, the Wisconsin head coach began asking me many questions about my football career and my work career. Then the head coach leaned over, put his arm around my neck, and very firmly and said to me, "Nick is coming to Wisconsin to play football, right!" All I could say at that point again is: "Yeahhh."

As I now realize, I had just learned College Recruiting 101. It is amazing, and to this day my friends know this story, and I use this tactic to be funny with my friends. The funny thing that Nick remembers is that the head coach was eating the Gardetto's snacks, but all he was eating were the rye chips, and he was crunching away as he talked. Such a big day, and that is what he remembers.

We continued the conversations with Wisconsin, and our high school head coach did inform the appropriate people at Michigan that Nick changed his mind and now wanted to go to Wisconsin to play football. Nick never wavered at all, and from that point Wisconsin was the team he wanted to play for.

Nick went into his senior year to play football. Nick was now 6 feet 4 inches tall and weighed 275 pounds. He had worked out extremely hard in the summer and this was his year to excel. During two a days in the beginning of the season, Nick came home one day early from football practice and was crying. I asked Nick what was going on. Nick stated his head football coach just kicked him out of practice. As any parent would do, I asked Nick why. Nick said because he didn't get a drink of water when they had a break from practice. I looked at Nick in amazement and said, "Nick, you do not get kicked out of practice for not getting a drink. What really happened?"

Nick continued to say, "Dad, that *is* what happened," and I was getting angrier every time he said it. All that was going through my head was that he was going to lose a potential scholarship. About an hour went by and, all of a sudden, the phone rang. I answered the phone, and it was his head football coach. All he said to me was could I meet him in his office at 8 a.m. tomorrow morning, and before I could ask why, he hung up. Now I was really furious and continued to ask Nick what was going on. Nick continued to say he had refused to get a drink of water. All I can say is that evening was not a very good evening; all I wanted to know was *why*.

The next morning I went to the coach's office. I do not get nervous often, but I do have to say this time I was a little nervous because I did not believe what Nick was saying, and now I was going to hear the truth. The coach asked me to sit down, and I did. The coach looked at me and said, "Bill, I have been trying to find something to make an example of Nick, and the kid does nothing wrong. He follows everything I tell him to do. Finally, yesterday, I told the kids to get some water, and Nick did not go. I told Nick, 'Go get water,' and he politely said he was fine. All I know is, I may not find anything that your son does wrong, so I took advantage of this and kicked him out of practice." The coach went on to say, "I just want the entire team know there are no superstars on the team and that we are all one team. I hope you do not mind that I made an example out of your son, and it was just to show everyone there are no superstars on this team."

What a Ride

I looked directly into the coach's eyes and told him he could do anything like that to my son to show this is a team. The coach looked at me and said, "I knew you would say that because of who you are." Honestly, I was so relieved to know Nick was telling the truth and that this was all about developing a team atmosphere, which both my wife and I are all about. This was another example why us moving to North Lake was such a great thing. I am all about the team, and it was so great to see a coach wanting to be the focus of the team.

The team was rated number one in state and one of the neatest things that year is both of my sons were on varsity. My younger son, Alex, was a sophomore and made the varsity team. Alex did not play a lot that year but it was nice to have them together and experience football together. We could see Alex growing and getting better all the time. It was such a great time in the Hayden household and all we could think about is: what a ride.

Nick had another great year and in one game played eight different positions on the field. It was so nice to see him play at a high level but always was a team player and never did I see the success go to his head. The team went through the season and again made it to the playoffs. The team won their first two games in the playoffs and was headed into the semi-final game to go back to the state championship. The opponent was Oak Creek, a team rated very high in state, too. One of my quarterbacks in college, who was also one of my roommates in college, came to the game. I was excited for him to come and watch my sons play. The Arrowhead team started out very slow and was not having a very good game. By the end of the third quarter, they were losing 25-7, and it looked like the game was over. I said to my friend from college, "I really appreciate you coming to the game, but it looks like our season is over." The Arrowhead players started to do many things right, and we started scoring. At the end, Arrowhead came back and won the game 26-25, and it was the biggest comeback I had seen at that point in football. It was so exciting, and we were so proud of our kids

Football in High School

Nick, Alex, and Abbey on the Arrowhead football field after a game

and we were going back to the state football championship for a second time in row.

That week leading up to the game was so much fun with so many school activities. We'd gone through this before so we knew what to expect. We did the same thing the day of the game. We saw all the football players off as they left on the bus to Madison. We again went up to Madison right away and spent the entire day in Madison before a 4 p.m. kickoff.

We all thought this was the year that Arrowhead would win the championship, but to our surprise, right from the beginning, the game was over. Our opponent came out and scored on us right away and many times, and it was never a close game. All you could do in the stands was watch and say we made it to state for a second year in a row, but both times we ended up taking second in state. It was a little easier to take this time around being through it once before, but it still hurt. Truly, the hardest thing now was that my son was a senior and this was the last game he would play as a high school football player.

There was one highlight to this game for me, and that was when Nick's coach received the second place state football trophy on the field, he received it from my high school coach. That was such a neat experience for me to see that and again another lesson on how those in my life playing football were now part of my son's life playing football. As sad as we were driving back to meet the football players at Arrowhead, my wife and I were so thankful for all that we had experienced with the Arrowhead football program through the last four years. We realized we still had our younger son playing for two more years in high school, and my older son was most likely going to play football in college.

To this day, I have to admit I still love watching high school football, and it's because the players are growing and always wanting to get better, they are so passionate about the game and are doing it because they love it, with no money attached to it. In addition, it is the friendships you make with the parents and all of the experiences you have with the parents. We were a very close-knit family at Arrowhead with so many great kids that played football and so many great parents who loved to be together and cheer for every football player on team. What a ride.

CHAPTER 3

THE AWARDS AND RECOGNITION

Now the season was over and some great things happened for Nick. He again made all-state as defensive lineman and defensive player of the year for two consecutive years. My wife and I were so proud of him. Nick had worked so hard so far in his career and the hard work had paid off. You learn that working hard does pay off in the end, and now having a son who was excelling in football by working hard was just such a great honor. Nick was now set to play football at Wisconsin. He was in contact with the coaches, and the official visit at Madison was set up. We went to Madison and the experience was even better than our Michigan experience. One of the neat moments was we were put up in a beautiful hotel, and when we walked in the room there was a giant football-shaped cookie on one of the beds, and Nick got an opportunity that night to go out with some current players to a Badgers basketball game.

We toured the football facilities and saw where Nick's locker was going to be, with a jersey with his name and number in the locker. Seeing that jersey really was a key point to realizing our son was going to play football for the Wisconsin Badgers. That day was such a memorable day, and it ended with dinner with all the other recruits who were receiving a scholarship and all of the coaching staff, the football staff, and their significant others. We had such a great evening. Mary and I were the last parents

What a Ride

to leave that night and stayed with all the coaches to the end. We knew at that point our son had made the right choice in schools, and it was our start to developing great relationships with his coaches.

Truthfully, we never really knew until that evening why Nick had made the switch from going to Michigan to Wisconsin, but learned why that day. The first reason was his position coach. Nick said there was a change with the position coach in Michigan, and when he had come to Madison for those three days, it was because the position coach at Madison had helped make the decision to play football at Wisconsin. After meeting with his position coach that day, I could see why. He was an upfront straight shooter who looked at both Mary and me and told us he would take care of Nick as if he were his own son. There was no reason not to believe he would do just that. I was so excited because I knew that was exactly what Nick needed at the next level. The other reason was that Nick wanted us to be able to see his games as well as continue to watch Alex play on Friday nights in high school. To us that was huge because we were able to do just that and continue to watch all of our children play in all of their games. The only thing to do was wait for signing day for the scholarship.

Well. it did not end there; Nick was selected to represent the State of Wisconsin at the All-American Bowl in San Antonio, Texas. Nick was the only football player in the state to be selected. This was such a big honor. Not only was my son an All-State football player, now he was an All-American football player in high school. This game was played on January 4. We were so blessed to be able to take our family to San Antonio for the week. This was on our dime of course but was a trip of a lifetime. We went down and stayed on the River Walk, which San Antonio is known for. We went to the practices and went to every event they had that week. We also spent a lot of time on the River Walk and before the All-American game that week they had a college bowl game. That in itself was so neat to see because every night on the River Walk tons of fans from the two

The Awards and Recognition

college teams were partying and chanting continuously for their team against each other across the river. The atmosphere was so great and truly pumped us up. We spent New Year's Eve in downtown San Antonio, and being from cold Wisconsin it was so great being outside and enjoying the festivities. At midnight, the town put on a fireworks show that was second to none. We were having such a great time with everything, and watching practice with the best players in the United States was just fabulous.

One of the great moments of that week was when my daughter, Abbey, who was around seven years old at the time, got into the elevator of our hotel while the biggest player ever (who, we were told, was also the biggest baby ever born in Louisiana) got in the elevator and stood right in front of my daughter Abbey. He concealed Abbey on the ride up the elevator, and I still remember my daughter saying as we exited the elevator, "Daddy, that is the biggest man I ever saw." He was 6 feet 9 inches tall and weighed 350 pounds. It was a moment to remember. I also remember a coach saying to us that week, "You will never see this caliber of football players together in one place or see such a highly talented game because all of these players are the top players in the United States." These were players like Adrian Peterson, Ted Ginn, and Chad Henne, and they all went to different colleges after this event.

After a great week of activities and fun, the game was finally here. Nick's coach in high school and his wife also came to the game, and this was such a big moment for his coach because he had coached so many great players in his career, but this was the first time he'd ever had a player in the All-American Bowl. This was also going to be the first time our son was going to be on national TV, and my wife and I were so humbled but very proud of our son's accomplishments.

I will tell you (and you will see this many times in this book) that these accolades and awards never went to my son's head. One of the things we have always heard about our son to this day from so many people is how down to earth Nick is, and he

WHAT A RIDE

Nick, #13, with teammates at the High School All-American game in San Antonio, Texas

never lets these types of things go to his head. One of the things Mary and I had said for the last seven years to our son is: this is the biggest game you are playing in. We started saying that in peewee league, in high school games, the state games, and now we were saying it to him again in the All-American Bowl. This was the biggest event that had ever occurred in our lives, and now I have a seventeen-year-old son playing in the biggest event in his life. Nick was selected to the All-American Bowl as a defensive lineman to play both defensive end and tackle. To our surprise, he was also going to play tight end that week because that was his main position on offense in high school. Nick was one of just a few players who played both ways in the game. That in itself was so great because you have all of the best players in the United States, and my son is one of the few to play both ways. What an honor that was.

    The game started and one of the things we'd heard from the coaches all week was that as spectators we were going to see some of the hardest hitting. The speed of the game was at such a high level, it was incredible. My son started at defensive tackle

The Awards and Recognition

and was making some nice tackles during the game. They really rotated the players in so that everyone got a chance to play.

During the second half of the game, they put Nick in as a tight end on offense. They were close to scoring, and on the next play the quarterback threw a pass to my son in the end zone and he caught it for a touchdown. If anyone would have told me that my son was going to catch a touchdown in this nationally televised game, I would have said, "Nick is playing defense, so that's not going to happen; you are crazy." However, he did, and I still remember being in the stands yelling that was my son who caught the ball. It was no doubt one of the biggest moments for all of us, to have a son play in that game on national TV and catch a touchdown. It is truly a moment I will never forget.

At the end of the game, Nick's team won, which made it that much more special. Who would have ever thought that when Nick was in sixth grade and I was saying, "I am blessed to have a healthy son," a son who was tripping over his own two feet as he started playing football, to now having a son who not only played in the biggest high school football game you can play in, but also caught a touchdown pass, and the team won. It was truly a big moment in our lives. What a ride.

Then the next big moment was on February 4, which coincidentally was Nick's eighteenth birthday; he signed his scholarship to play football at the University of Wisconsin and was now officially a Badger. Every event just seemed to continue to get bigger, and now I was going to have a son playing Division 1 football for the state he grew up in. This again was a dream come true, not only for Nick but for Mary and me.

Nick finished his senior year in high school, and things were going to start changing for him. The demands of a student athlete in college are much higher than they are in high school. This started immediately. Nick graduated from high school on a Sunday, and on the next day, Monday, he was heading to Madison for their summer program. There was no break for him, and it was the first time Nick was going to be away from home, from us. We were very excited for him, but also very sad when he left, because it was the start of not having all of our children at home.

We also bought Nick his first cellphone because now the only way to communicate on a regular basis was to call him. He began his workouts and met some new friends. Nick did not come home because of his workout schedule, and we did not see him until July when he also played in the state football game, which all the All-State football players play in. Usually the game is played at Titan Stadium in Oshkosh, Wisconsin, but because there were renovations being made to the stadium, the game was played at a local high school in Neenah-Menasha, Wisconsin. This would be the last time Nick would have any ties with high school, and it was such a big honor for him to be able to play with some of his teammates as well as other players he played against in high school and to make some new friends. It was a game where he could go out and play and just have fun. Nick did just that.

As a parent, though, I did have in the back of my mind that high school was over, and my son was going to have a chance to play football in college, and I did not want him to get injured in this game and cause issues with playing football in college. Injuries are always a concern, and Mary and I were always asked if we worried about injuries as our son played football. As I said, it was in the back of our mind, but it never really was a concern to us. Playing football myself, I knew that it was a chance you take. I was very fortunate in my career never to be injured, and I never missed a practice. Every athlete does receive minor injuries, like ankle sprains, broken fingers, minor concussions, but we always believed that people could be injured in so many ways in life, so this would not be a concern for us in sports. It may be a thought in your mind, but it never stopped us from having our kids play sports. In fact, our thought process was that no matter what happened, our kids were going to learn so many life lessons from playing sports, and if they had a career-ending injury, they would take life lessons even from that. Bottom line, in our opinion, life is just too short to worry about injuries.

The Awards and Recognition

Nick did get through the game injury-free and had so much fun and great memories from the event, and now it was time to prepare for playing football in college. We also believed it was important that our children play multiple sports because it helps you improve in all aspects of another sport. Some parents believe that specializing in one sport helps your game, but it really is important for your body to play different sports. We were very fortunate to have coaches at Arrowhead who also believed in this philosophy.

CHAPTER 4

Playing Football in College

The Wisconsin Badgers had built a winning tradition under their head coach. They had won the Rose Bowl in the nineties and were considered a top elite football program not only in the Big Ten but also in the nation. We were so excited for the next journey, and one of the first things we learned after Nick decided to play football at Wisconsin was that we could participate in so many things because Madison was an hour and fifteen minutes away. If Nick had gone to Michigan, every game would have been like an away game.

One of the things that Mary and I did right from the beginning and quite often all four years was attend many practices. There would have been no way that that could have occurred at Michigan. We loved the practices and to this day if someone asks what I miss the most, I can say it was the games, but second, it was the practices. The coaches encouraged parents to attend. They said it made the players practice harder. We enjoyed them because we could also see our son more and get to know the other players on the team, too. The players became part of our family and most knew who Mary and I were. One thing I never understood is why other parents never took advantage of this; it really was so much fun, and we did feel part of the Badger football family because of going to the practices. On the other hand, there were players who came from out of state, and so many parents not only did not go to practices, they missed many games. We really appreciated Nick deciding to stay in state and play football at Wisconsin. One of the first practices we went to was indoors because of inclement weather. I really enjoyed the inside practices the most because we were able to get so close to our son and watch him practice. On this day, we had our daughter Abbey with us, who was seven years old. We were watching practice and I had my video camera capturing Nick practice. Nick failed to do some proper technique, and his coach got all over him. I loved it, because being an athlete myself, I know that is all part of the game and will make you a better player.

One of the things I forgot, even though I loved it, was that I had my seven-year-old daughter standing in front of me and there was some swearing. All of a sudden, my daughter Abbey tugged on my pants, looked at me, and said, "Daddy, Daddy, there is a lot of swearing that goes on." Well it was an eye opener to her, and until she got into sports, she did experience some of these things, as she went everywhere with us. To this day, I have taught my kids one big lesson about coaches, and that is that when a coach is yelling at you, all they want you to do is get better because they care about you and want you to succeed. When you have to worry is when a coach stops yelling or giving you constructive feedback, because that is when they may have given up on you. Some people may not agree with this, but it is something that has been ingrained with my family and has helped my children get through some hard times when trying to understand the why.

One of the other things I would like to mention is that the other big positive of Nick deciding to go to Madison was that we were able to see both Nick play in college as well as seeing my younger son Alex play football in high school. As I stated earlier, this was also one of the reasons Nick selected Wisconsin over Michigan and really shows the great character of my son thinking of the family.

As a freshman, Nick was becoming acclimated on the team. There were some great defensive linemen on the team,

WHAT A RIDE

Nick, #96, during a Badger game against Indiana University

and the coaches did not know in the beginning if they would redshirt Nick or not. There is a time period to decide this in the beginning of the season. It was not until the end of that period that the coaching staff decided not to redshirt him. The reason, they told us, is that Nick was progressing along very well and they wanted to get him in the games to get some real action because they thought he would be a big contributor for next year. That is exactly what happened. Nick played his freshman year in football and it was not a lot, but he did get time in games that gave him a flavor of what was needed to become a major contributor on the team.

That year Nick grew tremendously as a football player. Nick came in to the program weighing about 260 pounds. Nick put on 45 pounds during the summer strength and conditioning program and now weighed 305. It was amazing to see how his body transformed from high school to college. The weight program at Wisconsin was phenomenal, and you really could see the difference in Nick. Nick played with so many talented football players, and every starter on the defensive line that year made it to the NFL. Nick was fitting in well with the team and his position coach.

Playing Football in College

There's nothing like going to a Badger game. The stadium was just renovated and was beautiful. The pregame activities are phenomenal. We tailgated every home game. We found a spot that we shared with another family from our high school whose son was a quarterback on the team. We tailgated at the same spot for all four years at Wisconsin. My wife was big into the tailgating. Every game with the two families, we would have seventy to a hundred people at our tailgates. There were always a lot of the same families and friends, but each time others would come, too. We would always bring a lot of beer and liquor, and my wife would always make a big dish of something like chili or barbecue for everyone who attended. Others would bring a dish to pass around, so there was always enough food and alcohol for all.

Tailgating was a big part of the game. We would get to a game two to three hours early, set up our tailgate, and enjoy family and friends before the game. We would always go down to the arch of the stadium to see Nick get off the bus and wish him an excellent game. We would then pack everything back up in the cars for the game, and after the game we would come back and tailgate for another three to four hours. Those were long days, but never once did it feel long, and we always wanted to do the tailgate parties. There are so many memories from the tailgate parties, and being with family and friends during these four years was awesome. After every game Nick would come to the tailgate party with a bunch of his teammates, and that was always so special because it was another time we would be able to see him. As an athlete, you are so busy with school, studying, weightlifting, practices, and games that we cherished the times we got to see him. The games again were the highlight, and being in the stadium on game day is an experience we will remember for the rest of our lives.

To see the sea of red in the stands is so neat. To see your son come out of the tunnel gave us shivers every time. That never went away. The different activities that go on during the game are incredible. Things like the jump around after the third quarter, Bucky doing push-ups after each time they scored, the student section and all the different activities they do during the game, and the "fifth quarter," when the band plays for a period of time after each game.

In addition to all these activities, we learned very quickly that Wisconsin did some things that did not happen in other stadiums at the time. The first thing is that they show a replay for every down. This may seem trivial, but when you have a son playing, I loved to watch it live and then be able to see it on the replay on the big screen. The reason is because your eyes are glued on your son to see if he does his job or makes a play or not, and then you can watch the play on the big screen as a whole. It does make a big difference. The other thing is that there were so many activities on the big screen as entertainment during the game.

One of my favorite was when they would ask players a question and they would show several different players answering the question. It was always so hilarious and because we knew so many players, it did make you feel more part of the football family. The scoreboard also kept you informed of everything for the game and on the games going on throughout the country. I can say that having traveling to all the Big Ten schools and many other colleges where they played, Wisconsin was by far the best in this category. I know I am a little biased about this, but after seeing so many stadiums and the atmosphere outside and inside the stadiums, I do have to admit Wisconsin was number one in this category.

I think the only other thing that was great to see was when the band dots the "i" at Ohio State or seeing a game at Penn State in which everyone wears white in the stadium, which is called the "White Out." The stadium looked so clean and just like seeing the red in the Badger stadium, seeing the "White Out" looks so awesome to me.

In Nick's sophomore year, he went through spring football practice and was slotted to be the starting defensive of tackle in the fall. It was such an exciting time in our lives because our son had a chance to be a starter for such a great football program. That fall during training camp before the season started, my wife and I were at an outdoor practice watching Nick and the entire team. During drills, Nick was in with the first team practicing their defense playing against the offense. We were proud parents on the sidelines, and all of a sudden, after a play, Nick's position coach runs out in the field and tells Nick to get on the sidelines if he can't do what he is supposed to do on the play. That is a hard thing to watch. It was especially hard for my wife because this is her son, her baby, and now he is being yelled at and pulled off the field. No more than fifteen seconds after his coach did this, he ran over to us as we stood on the sidelines and says to Mary and me, "Hey, I tell you what, you two take care of Nick off the field, and I will take care of Nick on the field."

It was such a powerful moment for me because of my past sports career, but to my wife this was her baby and she did not like it. I gave the coach thumbs-up and said that makes sense to me. My wife stayed silent, which I understood because of the mother-son relationship. That evening one of the reporters had asked my son's coach about Nick being pulled out, and he said to the reporter, "I talked to the parents right after that incident, and I have their permission to take care of their son on the field, and they are going to take care of him off the field."

For most people this may not seem like a big deal, but I did remember what the coach had told us when we met with him before Nick selected Wisconsin. He'd said that he would take care of our son just like Nick was his own son. After the incident that day and reading the article, I knew that my son was going to be coached by a great coach.

Nick did become the starter, and watching my son in his first start was such a special moment. It was a dream come true for him and for us, and he was having such a great year and so was the entire Badger team.

As good as the home games are, the away games are just as special. During away games, depending where it was, we'd either go to the game the day of or would go to the location the night before. We would either tailgate at the game or, more often than not, we would just go to a bar before a game with friends and family. We had bought this conversion van to take to the away games. Friends and family would always go with us in the van.

I have a close friend who played football through college and always came to the high school football games to see my sons play. He came to almost all the Badger games, too. With all my children in sports and both my wife and I working full time, it was a very busy time. We loved every moment of it and always went to all of our kids' activities.

One of the most memorable moments was in one weekend when we did not miss any of our children's activities. You may say that is not such a big deal, but this was not an ordinary weekend. On Friday night after working all week, we went to the Friday night high school football game to watch my younger son, Alex, play. The games always started at 7 p.m. and would go until around 9:30 p.m. We finished watching that game, congratulated Alex on his performance, and we (I, my friend, and our wives) got in the van right after the game and headed to see my other son, Nick, play the next day at Penn State. We drove all night, taking turns driving. This is about a twelve-hour drive from Wisconsin. We got to the stadium around 11:00 a.m. and the game was at 2:30. We were going to just all take a nap until the game, but when we got in the parking lot there was so much tailgating going on around us we just joined in and tailgated until the game started.

We then went to the game, and after the game saw our son and again congratulated him on a great game, and then got back into the van and started driving home again. We left at about 7 p.m., and again it was about a twelve-hour drive home. We all took turns driving and were coming home again because my daughter, Abbey, had a swim meet from 9 a.m. to 5 p.m. on Sunday. We got home around 8 a.m. in the morning, dropped our friends at their home, came home and picked up Abbey, and went to her swim meet (which was local) all day. We came

Playing Football in College

home ate a little, went to bed, and both my wife and I went to work in the morning.

As hard as this was, it was well worth it, and we were able to see all of our kids participate in their sports that weekend. We did this type of thing repeatedly and enjoyed every minute of it. To this day, there is nothing more special for us than watching our kids play sports or any activities they may do. This was our life and we were taking advantage of it all.

That same year Wisconsin played Michigan in Madison, and it was going to be a big game for us because again Nick was originally going to play for Michigan and then decided to go to Wisconsin. There was one hiccup. Both of my sons were going to play at the same time that day. My younger son, Alex, who was a senior in high school, was playing on a Saturday evening, and as you know, most games are played on Friday nights in high school, so this was an exception. My wife and I had always tried to attend almost all of our children's activities, and now we had a conflict, with both of them playing at the same time. My wife and I talked about what to do and decided we would ask Alex if it was okay if we went to the game in Madison, since it was against Michigan. Being the child Alex is, he said, "No problem, Mom and Dad. I understand. And anyways, the team we are playing isn't that good, and us starters will probably only play the first half of the game."

It still was hard not being able to see both of them play, but I have to admit we were excited for our son that day because of the correlation with Michigan. Every game is a bigger game in my son's career and this was no exception.

One of the nice things about being the dad is you can always give your sons the motivational talks before each game. I had done this through their football careers, and this day was no exception. Because it was a night game, we got to Madison early in the afternoon and started tailgating. It was time for the game, and we closed the tailgate and went into the stadium. All we wanted was for our son to play well against the team he was originally going to play for and to beat them as a team. This was such an exciting game, and Nick did have a great game that day, and we did beat Michigan.

I remember right after the game, dancing in the stands saying, "I am going to party all night long," to everyone around us. We had some good friends with us, and Mary decided to go with her girlfriend to meet Nick as he came out of the locker room. I said I would go back to the tailgate and get everything out of the car with my friend. As soon as I got out of the stadium, my phone rang. I thought maybe it was someone calling me to congratulate me about Nick having a great game and beating Michigan. It was not that type of call; it was a call that no parent wants to receive. It was the athletic director of our high school calling, and the first words out of his mouth were, "You need to get home as soon as possible."

I asked him why. He said, "Alex is nonresponsive."

I said to him, "What do you mean Alex is nonresponsive?"

The athletic director said, "All I can tell you is that during the football game Alex collapsed and he is nonresponsive, and they took him to Children's Hospital in Wauwatosa."

It is the worst feeling ever not to know what is going on, and also Mary went one way and I another, and we were not together at a point of a true emergency. I just went from the highest high—one of our sons having such a great game in college football—to the lowest of lows, with our other son being nonresponsive and not knowing what that meant. I literally ran back to where our car was parked for tailgating and tried to call Mary, and it was not going through. I got to the lot where our car was located, and, thank God, Mary was running to the car, too. Our athletic director was able to get hold of Mary, and she, too, got the bad news.

As you might imagine, Mary was extremely upset because all we knew was that our son was nonresponsive. We always were the first to get to the tailgate and usually the last to leave and so never had to worry about being blocked in by other cars. This day was different, and all I could think about was how we were going to be able to get out of the lot with so many cars

Playing Football in College

blocking us in. Somehow, everyone returned and we were able to move enough cars to get out of the lot and start heading home. If you've ever left a major sporting event right after a game, you know that there is a lot of traffic. This was no exception, and we were now stuck in traffic, moving very slowly.

Two of our good friends came with us, and it was such a blessing because while I was driving they were consoling Mary. The one time you need a cop to help you in life there are none to be seen. It took us an hour to get out of Madison and another hour to get to the hospital, and all we knew during that time is that our son was nonresponsive. We did get two calls from the athletic director on the way home, but they were nothing but courtesy calls and the only thing he would say is, "Alex is still nonresponsive." We finally arrived at the hospital and walked in. In the waiting room were so many players and their parents. It was truly amazing that during a crisis like this how supportive people can be and to see everyone in that waiting room because of my son's condition was something I will never forget.

We then met with the doctor, who explained to us that Alex had the highest-level concussion and what appeared to be a spinal concussion and was currently paralyzed from the waist down. The doctor said he was unconscious at the time, and both my wife and I asked if we could see him. The doctor took us to the room and they had Alex's arms strapped to the bed with leather straps. We asked why the straps, and the doctor said it was to prevent him from removing the tube that was opening his airway to breathe. To see your son like this was a parent's nightmare. They did not know exactly what had happened at that time, but all that was known was he collapsed on the sidelines and stopped breathing and they had to put the tube in to open his airway on the sidelines.

The doctor said now it will just take time to see what will happen. It was around 12:30 a.m., and Mary and I stayed at his bedside until around 3:30 a.m. One of the things the doctor told us was to continue to talk to him, that this can help to bring him back. The nurse finally came in and said that they had prepared a room for us to sleep in, right next to the room Alex was in, and that they would come get us if there was any change. Both Mary and I said to Alex that we were going to get some sleep in the next room, and all of a sudden Alex came to and was so strong he broke the leather straps and was trying to pull the tube out of his mouth. I yelled for the nurse for help, and she came in the room and just told me to try to hold him down. I told the nurse he was trying to pull the tube out of his throat.

Alex continued to fight and the nurse finally called a doctor on the phone. The nurse was given permission to remove the tube, but they had to now monitor him with other medical machines to make sure he did not stop breathing. Once they removed the tube, Alex became nonresponsive again. The whole incident was so bizarre—seeing someone nonresponsive then become agitated and do what he did and then become nonresponsive again. All we knew was that somewhere in his brain he knew we were going to leave and he did not want the tube down his throat.

After everything settled down, the nurse again told us to get some sleep and she would get us if anything changed. Mary and I did get a couple hours of sleep and then we got back up and started talking to Alex as the doctor said to do. Both Mary and I were telling him stories from his past and just kept talking. That day so many players, coaches, and parents came to see Alex. Again, the doctor encouraged this and wanted everyone who visited to keep talking to Alex. It was good for Alex to hear others talk, and this could help him come back from being nonresponsive. The entire day went by, and so many things went through my head about my son, and not knowing what could come next. In the early evening, a miracle happened, and it happened very quickly. Alex started to come to. The doctor was called in, and he said, "Keep talking to him."

We did just that, and Alex started to blurt things out, saying things like, "My brother plays football." He could say his name and was talking about his sister. We kept asking him questions, and he was fuzzy, but he would keep saying things. Some of it

Playing Football in College

Alex, #71, with his girlfriend, now wife, wearing his jersey after an Arrowhead football game

was not making sense, but he was talking. It took about an hour and Alex was back. It happened that fast.

What a relief to Mary and me. We had our son back. Alex began to get his feeling back in his lower body and everything was looking good. He stayed in the hospital for another couple days for observation and was released from the hospital. Per doctor's orders, Alex could not play football until further notice. We had doctor's appointments weekly for Alex. We did not know if football was over for Alex, not only this year but also Alex had an opportunity to play at the next level, so his football career could be over for good.

After the incident, Alex was progressing nicely every week with no side effects. After the third week, we asked the doctor if Alex would be able to play this year again. The doctor said let's wait one more week to decide that. We came back the following week and the doctor asked Alex if he wanted to play again. Alex said, "Yes, we are going to be in the playoffs, and I want to play." Now as a parent, after experiencing what we just went through with our son, the question becomes do you let him play. Alex said he wanted to play, and that is no doubt the competitive side of all of us; but do we want to chance a similar situation again? This was a hard decision, but we went back to the fact the doctor had released him to play and that, again, anyone could get injured almost doing anything in life, and we let Alex decide and his decision was to play. I am not sure how other parents felt, and I am sure some thought we were crazy, but game day came for the first playoff game, and Alex was suited up.

Alex was a previous starter as a left offensive tackle (which was the same position I played in high school and college), but Alex did not start this game. I do not know why, but I am sure the coach could have been a little concerned because of how serious the situation was, and he had seen it. In the beginning of the second quarter, the offense went out on the field, and Alex was running out with them. I have to admit my heart did drop, and it was in my head, thinking, *Are we doing the right thing?* This is no lie. The stands went completely quiet. You could have heard a pin drop.

The lineman ran up to the line of scrimmage, and I heard the quarterback say, "Hike." Alex took off and literally plowed the defensive lineman over and ran right over him. The problem was, Alex was the only one who'd moved. The play was to be on the second "hike," and Alex had jumped offsides. All of a sudden, all you heard in the stands was everyone clapping and yelling, "Way to go, Alex!"

There are not too many instances when you can jump offsides and get a round of applause from the spectators, but Alex did that day. It was amazing. I am sure it took the butterflies away, and Alex played the rest of the game and had a fantastic game. They went on to the next level of the playoffs, and Alex started again and had another great game. Unfortunately, the team lost, and this was the end of Alex's high school football career.

However, my college team at Whitewater was recruiting Alex. This was very exciting because as big a deal as it was having a son play for the Wisconsin Badgers, it was also as exciting that I might have a son play football where I played. The head coach at Whitewater was the quarterback coach when I'd played, and

Playing Football in College

he had really taken the football program to the next level. Alex and I began visiting the coach and the Whitewater campus.

Nick was having a great sophomore year on the field and so was the team. The team was ranked high in the nation, and we ended up getting a January 1 bowl game again, the Capital One Bowl in Orlando, Florida. The Bowl games are special not only for the players, but also for the parents. One of my favorite spots to vacation is Florida, and this was exciting that we were going to play in Florida. We did take a week vacation with all of our family that year and enjoyed the warmth on the beach as well as spending Christmas in Florida.

The team also went down a week before to practice and to get ready for the game. There are also daily activities that the players do and activities that the parents can watch. We took advantage of everything. Because we knew so many parents, we would spend time with them during the week and it was like being one big family. The game was played in the Orlando Football Stadium, and it was another experience to be in that stadium. I can say that life does not get better than what we were experiencing.

The season was over and Nick was performing at a very high level, and he did receive All-Big Ten honorable mention as a defensive tackle. We could not believe it. It was again a dream come true and a very exciting time in our life, not only having one son playing in college but the following year possibly having two sons playing college football. We were truly on top of the world.

My younger son, Alex, was a wrestler. He was going into his senior year of wrestling after football. Alex approached me before the season started and said to me he did not want to wrestle his senior year and just wanted to work out and get ready to try to play football in college. I did not understand. I also had wrestled in high school, and wrestling really was a great complement to playing football and to help stay in shape. Finally, Alex said to me that he was only wrestling for me. I was smart enough after hearing this to understand that playing a

Alex on left, ready for his opponent during an Arrowhead wrestling match

sport cannot be for the parent; it must be for them. I realized I had pushed Alex hard both in football and wrestling and especially wrestling because there weren't many heavyweights to practice with, so I would go up to practice and wrestle with Alex.

I also knew he'd just gone through a major injury that season in football, and even though he never stated it, this may have contributed to him not wanting to wrestle. The bottom line is you have to play a sport for yourself—not a parent or anyone else. I looked at Alex and said to him, "OK. I understand, and you are lucky you told me before the season started because if it were during the season, I would have had a harder time with this."

I told Alex he was going to have to tell his wrestling coach that he did not want to wrestle his senior year. I never had to do this, but I did know it was the proper way and also I knew this would probably be hard to do. The wrestling coach was an excellent coach, and I knew he was counting on Alex to wrestle. Alex did tell his coach and did not wrestle his senior year.

I saw his coach several months later at a local festival. He came up to me and said, "Bill I was not happy that Alex did not

Playing Football in College

want to wrestle his senior year; we needed him on the team. However, I will say I am impressed with him coming to tell me. That really showed me his character." The coach said that he'd been coaching for twenty-five years and only a few people who quit ever came to him to tell him. Usually they just do not show up anymore. He then said, "You and Mary really have taught your son right."

As small as this may seem, it was a compliment to us as a family, and it is what we had tried to instill in all our kids. As hard as it was hearing that my son did not want to wrestle anymore and that he was only doing it for me, talking to his coach that day did put closure and a successful conclusion to that situation because it is about character in life. Alex did consistently work out that year in the weight room and was preparing to play football at the next level.

At the end of Nick's sophomore year, the head coach of Wisconsin decided to step down from coaching. He was a unique coach in that he took a position with Wisconsin as the athletic director two years before and continued to be the head coach, too. Now he was going to step down from coaching and only do his responsibilities as the athletic director. He had groomed another assistant coach, who now became the head coach for the Wisconsin Badgers. It was nice that they'd stayed within the team and did not look outside. A coaching change can be very difficult for some players who fit in the old scheme but may not in the new scheme. I even had a similar experience at a company that was sold; the new company brought in its own managers, and it can be very rough for certain people.

Nick was coming off a very good year, and we just hoped the change would not affect our son. Spring ball came and there were some changes on the defensive scheme. Nick weighed as much as 325 pounds his sophomore year and he was known as The Plugger in the middle under the old scheme and was very successful at it. Under the new scheme, they wanted Nick to shoot the gaps more. This was new to Nick, and he had to make some changes but maintained his weight at 325 pounds.

What a Ride

I was also spending time with my younger son, Alex, going to spring practices at Whitewater with him and getting back to where I played football in college felt great. Alex was asked to try out for the football team and in the end decided to attend Whitewater to go to school but not to try out for football team. The injury he'd received playing football in high school weighed heavily on him, and he'd decided that he wanted to just concentrate on his schooling and did not want to play football in college. Again, he had to tell the head coach this and to me this even had to be harder on him because I had played for that coach many years earlier.

These situations are real things you go through, and you realize how different circumstances can create different outcomes with your children. I have to say, I was disappointed and was a little selfish because I was so excited that I had a son who was going to play football where I had played college football. However, this is real life, and we were excited our son was going to college because both Mary and I dreamed and did push to have our children graduate from college. Alex not playing football was something we just had to accept, and we did accept it and truly were glad that Alex was healthy after the situation that happened in high school.

We still were very busy because our youngest child, Abbey, was now playing many different sports and we were excited for Nick's junior year in football. Having a full year as a starter and coming in this year as the starter we were very excited to see how he would progress. The team was rated high in the nation again and we wanted to cherish every moment because it was going so fast. These are times you never want to end, because you are on top of the mountain, experiencing something not every parent gets to. The team was doing really well and we again played Michigan, but this time in their stadium. We had several friends who wanted to attend this game because Nick was originally going to Michigan and to see the stadium that holds the most people in college football. We packed our van with friends and took off on a Friday afternoon to Ann Arbor.

Playing Football in College

We got to our hotel room and decided to go out to a local bar that night to have some fun before the game on Saturday. We were in the bar having some drinks and there was a radio station announcer who was announcing on the radio inside the bar. Because we are proud parents, we were wearing a pin with Nick's football picture on it. We did this in high school, and college was the same way. We were wearing Nick's pin that night in the bar. During the evening, the radio announcer said that the station was giving away two free tickets for tomorrow's game, and you could put your name in a basket to win them.

Now we all had tickets, but Mary and I for some reason went up and put our names in the basket. All of a sudden, the radio announcer looks at us, sees the pin with Nick's football picture on it and says, "Are you Nick Hayden's parents?" We say yes, and now he is on the radio telling everyone, "Hey, we have Nick Hayden's parents here. This is unbelievable." He started asking Mary a ton of questions about Nick, and my wife was hamming it up with him on the radio. I could not understand why he kept talking about Nick and was asking Mary all these questions. The radio announcer finally went on a commercial break, and I asked him just that. "Why are you asking so many questions about our son?" He said, "You don't know? Your son is a legend around here. Do you know he is the only player to ever de-commit from Michigan?" This was unbelievable, and he went back on the radio and continued to talk about Nick and how we were in the bar. We had no idea about this, and I have to admit we enjoyed every minute of this, and Mary was so good at answering all of his questions.

You could tell the radio announcer really liked Mary, and she was hamming it up very well with him. That night was a very special night for us, and we did have a lot of fun at the bar. It was time to go home and get ready for tomorrow's game. The game was at 2:30 p.m. and was a nationally televised game.

We got up and wanted to park close to the stadium so we could tailgate. We drove to the stadium and found parking at a golf course that was right across the street from the stadium.

WHAT A RIDE

We parked right on the golf course green. I could not believe we had our conversion van on the golf course green, and it was by far the best parking spot we'd ever had.

We set up camp and began to tailgate. We had probably thirty friends in our group and were having a great time. We again were wearing Nick's pin on our shirts. All of a sudden, a guy with a long pole with a mic on it came over and saw that we were wearing Nick Hayden's pin. He said to us, "Are you Nick's parents?" We said yes, and he looked at Mary and said, "The radio announcer really enjoyed talking with you last night. Say something to the announcer in the mic." Mary, being the person she is, said in a seductive voice, "Hey, thank you for last night. I really had a great time." He said, "This is great; he will love what you just said," and then ran off.

About ten minutes later that same person came running up to us and said, "Hey, the radio announcer would like you two to come to a tent by the stadium where he is doing a pregame show. You can come in and have all the beer and food you want, and he would like to talk to you again on the radio." My good friend who has come to every football game with us said to me, "Do you mind if I come, too? This is going to be great." I said yes and the three of us proceeded to the tent. We got wristbands and walked in, and immediately the radio announcer saw us and announced on the radio that "Nick Hayden's parents are in the tent." He again goes on about Nick and started asking Mary a bunch of questions again. He referred to her as "Nick Hayden's mom," and again Mary was hamming it up with him.

The radio announcer went on a commercial break, and he asked Mary if she would like to play football trivia on the radio. Of course Mary said yes. Mary gets up on the stage, sits down next to him, and on the other side of the radio announcer is her opponent, an All-American Hockey player from Michigan.

I cannot believe this is happening on the radio, and it is all because my son decided not to play football at Michigan. The radio announcer kept referring to Mary as "Nick Hayden's mom," and he asks the Michigan Hockey player a football trivia question. He gets it wrong and he turns to Mary and asks her the same question. Well, they have another person next to Mary whispering the answers to her and she gets it right. The radio announcer says, "Hey, everybody, Nick Hayden's mom got it right; she knows her football."

This went on, and Mary won the trivia contest against the Michigan All-American Hockey player, which was unbelievable. The radio announcer then announced on the radio that "Nick Hayden's mom has won a cooler with beer with a bunch of T-shirts and hats."

I was so happy for Mary that she was getting some radio time because of this situation, knowing it would be a cherished memory forever. We then left the tent, went back to our tailgate with the winnings and prizes, and told the story of what just happened to all of our friends. The game had not even started, and everything that had happened within such a short period was incredible.

We went to the game, and the stadium was beautiful. We had seen the stadium from the head coach's office when Nick was being recruited, but being in the stadium was even better. Unfortunately, we did lose the game, but it was a hard-fought game. Nick played extremely well again against Michigan, as he did his sophomore year.

We then went home, and like every game, a friend of ours had taped the game on TV for us. We always watched the game when we got home, and during this game they'd interviewed Nick on national TV. Mary had just had something so amazing happen to her during our visit, but now on national TV Nick was asked to tell the viewers something that no one would ever believe about him. Nick said, "I have wrestled my dad hundreds of times in my life, and he has pinned me every time. I have never beaten my dad in wrestling."

This was my special moment on national TV because it was true, and for him to say something like that about me on national TV was truly a special moment. There was no doubt this game was the highlight for Mary and me during Nick's

WHAT A RIDE

college football career, and I can say I have told this story hundreds of times in my life.

It was another great season, the team played in another January 1 Bowl in Florida, and again it was the Capital One Bowl in Orlando, Florida. Nick had a good season. There was no doubt with the coaching change and having his position coach change it became a learning season for him. If I had to compare his sophomore year with his junior year, he had a better season his sophomore year. Nick did not receive any conference awards his junior year, but did start every game and now had twenty-six starts under his belt. This year our family took advantage of having another bowl game in Florida, and we took a two-week vacation and spent time in different cities in Florida and again the last thing we did was go to the bowl game before heading back home to Wisconsin. Nick did have a great bowl game and the team won.

Now that Nick's junior year in football was complete, there was talk about the NFL. From his coaches there was discussion that Nick could go to the next level. There are never any guarantees but it was exciting that this was a possibility. I think we all knew, including Nick, that he would have to improve and have a very solid senior year for this to be a reality. I would talk to Nick about making sure he was working harder than ever in the off-season. Nick had always been a hard worker, but to make it to the pros he would need to dig in, lose some weight, get in the best shape of his life, and continue to improve, which Nick did. This is something I learned throughout my college career. If you do not improve every single year, you will not make it. A good example is when I was in college we had many all-state players my first year. By the time they were sophomores, they did not make the team because they plateaued and did not get better and did not make the team that year. This was always a concern of mine about Nick and when does he finally plateau. Nick wanted to make it to the pros and told me he was working hard to accomplish just that.

Playing Football in College

That same off-season, Whitewater was coming off a Division 3 National Championship. As excited as I was for the team that I had played for, there was still an emptiness, because my younger son, Alex, could have been on that team but decided not to go out. One day in the off-season I got a call from Alex that the offensive line coach approached him and asked him to reconsider going out for the team. Alex said he'd thought about it and now having a year under his belt was ready to try it. I was so excited because I thought Alex's career in football was over, and now he was going to try out again.

That year Alex was at spring football practice with the team. During his first week of practice, Alex hurt his back, and when he went to the doctor he was told it was in his best interest to give up football. The game can be so frustrating, and injuries are such a big part of football. I never got any major injuries, and my oldest son was injury-free so far in his football career, but Alex was not as lucky. Well, that was truly the end of Alex's football career, and I am just happy today that I have a healthy son who gave it his all. The ironic thing is Alex would have been on the team that took three national championships and came in second one time in what was his four years at Whitewater. What a ride.

CHAPTER 5

SENIOR YEAR IN COLLEGE

Things were moving fast in our lives. This was now Nick's last year in college; my daughter Abbey was starting to get involved with select sports, playing both basketball and volleyball, and we were trying to take it all in.

Nick again was starting at defensive tackle for the Wisconsin Badgers. Nick had trimmed down to 305 pounds, and was stronger and faster than ever. Nick knew this was his year both as a leader on the team and as a football player. There was more talk about him going to the pros. Mary and I had to go through some training about the NFL and things you can do and not do during this time. The coaches met with us and said that we would start getting calls from agents and asked us to take the lead on this and let Nick play football and enjoy his senior year. I had no problem with this and was excited to go through this process.

The coaches were right. We started to get several calls from agents. It really starts to get overwhelming because so many agents call and you do not know whom to select or what to do with trying to get the right ones to visit with you. One of the things we were told to do was meet with parents who had gone through the process before. We had a player from the Badgers the year before who was drafted in the first round of the NFL. I called the parents and asked if they would help me with the

Senior Year in College

agent process. The father said yes. I probably spent a total of 6 to 8 hours with him, learning the agent process, including what to do and not do with the agent. There was so much to learn, but more important, we wanted the right agent who would help our son in the NFL.

The first step was to select a few and start meeting with them. That is exactly what Mary and I did. We found that there are two types of agents. One type will tell you everything you wanted to hear, how they would help your son improve his draft level; the other type of agent seemed more realistic and told you how they would help your son if he made it to the NFL. This was the easy part, and we started meeting with agents who were in the second category.

I did have a couple of phone interviews where I had to hang up on the agent because he was rude during our discussion, telling me I knew nothing and needed his help. These agents were not the ones we wanted to deal with, so we would tell them that. We did come up with a list of around seven agents. We met with them at our house throughout the upcoming months. Each one would come prepared in different ways and would show us how they would help our son. We did learn a little from each one, and then, when the next one visited, we began to have more questions to ask. We wanted to learn as much as we could for our son and make sure we had found several agents for him to meet and pick from.

Early on in the process, we began to figure out which ones may be a good fit. One of the things Mary and I said right from the beginning was that our job was to bring several good agents to Nick so that he could select the one he thought was the best for him. Mary and I did not tell Nick which agents we thought were the best, so that it was truly his decision in the end. As we started interviewing them, it became clear which ones came to the top and would be good for our son. As much as it was fun to meet with all of these agents, it does become very time consuming, and with so many activities with our other kids, too, we were spending a lot of time on this, and we realized why the coaches had asked us to do this for Nick. After spending several months meeting with the agents, Mary and I did narrow it down to five agents.

After going through the process we discovered that Mary had a favorite agent and I had a different favorite agent. We promised to keep our favorites to ourselves and not tell Nick. We presented the list to Nick in mid-October of his senior year of college. Nick immediately was able to narrow it down to three agents. This was the first time we really saw Nick start making some logical decisions about his possible future in the NFL. We were seeing a maturity we had not seen before. This twenty-year-old kid was going to be forced into making some lifelong decisions, and we were happy to see how he was handling himself.

Nick was having a great senior year in football and for the fourth year in a row the team was rated high in the nation. There was speculation that Nick would go in the third or fourth round of the NFL draft. We never dreamed all the things that were happening, and it was so exciting, but we always tried to stay level-headed during this process, realizing that until it happens anything could happen.

It was the last home game and it was Parents' Day. We had our entire family, including grandparents, at the game. Before the game, all parents and relatives of the senior players go out on the field to greet all the players as they come out of the tunnel. Then, one by one, the senior players came out, greeted their families, then walked to the center of the field, and are recognized. It is such a big moment for us as a family but also one of the saddest moments because you know this part of your life is ending.

The Parents' Day game was against Michigan, and as I have told my son hundreds of times before, I said it again: "Son, this is going to be your biggest game ever." This was the last time he was going to play Michigan, and he had to show them who Nick Hayden was and how important of a win this was, not only for the team but also for himself. I told Nick that he had to give it

Senior Year in College

his all and have a great game and help the team win. I am not saying it was because of my speech, but Nick did have one of his best games against Michigan, sacking the quarterback several times and on many tackles. The Badgers won the game, and Nick could say that he beat the team two out of the three times they met. This was big for him (and us), knowing he made the right decision, and this just put the icing on the cake.

As with anything, there is an end, and it was extremely sad that this was the last home game for us being part of the Wisconsin Badgers family. We had so many memories and so much fun; we did not want it to ever end. We knew that we possibly had some more football coming up, but we also knew how hard it is to get into the NFL, so you do not take anything for granted. We just wanted to cherish the moment and we all did. We were very proud of Nick's accomplishments, and that day on the field was a day that no one in my family ever forgot. What a ride.

The season was over and the Badgers were going to the Outback Bowl on January 1 in Tampa, Florida. We were so excited for the game, but now we had a lot of work in front of us, with Nick getting prepared for the NFL. The week of Thanksgiving, Nick had off, before starting practice again for the Bowl game. We took advantage of this because Nick was at home with us. We scheduled three interviews with the three agents Nick had decided he would meet. One on Monday, one on Tuesday, and one on Wednesday. Because Mary and I each had our favorites, I did schedule the one that was neither of our favorites first; then, I have to admit, I scheduled Mary's favorite second and my favorite last. Nick again did not know who we wanted. I will say all three were very good, and Mary and I were very glad that Nick was happy with who we presented to him.

On Monday, the first agent came to our house and visited with Nick. The agent knew this was his one shot at representing Nick, so he came in with a lot of information and details about what he would do for our son. Nick was asking many questions, but you could tell it was a lot for him to handle. We cannot forget

WHAT A RIDE

he was only twenty years old and was making probably one of the biggest decisions of his life. This was literally a five-hour meeting. We finally got the agent to leave, and I still remember Nick saying, "I am done with this; it is too much."

We knew Nick needed to go through the other two interviews, and all we could tell him was just that and then it will be over. The next two nights were the same way, and they are five-hour meetings. It was a lot but what a great experience to go through. We were done and all Nick needed to do was make a decision. Well, it was not an easy decision for Nick.

The next day was Thanksgiving, and like every Thanksgiving, we have many relatives over. Thanksgiving is my wife's favorite holiday, and she enjoys making the food and having everyone over. It was our tradition. Well, this one was a little different because everyone wanted to ask Nick questions about the agents and wanted him to make a decision about who he was going with. I am sure it was a long day for Nick, and he kept telling everyone he had not made a decision and wanted to think on it for a while. It was definitely not what everyone wanted to hear, including Mary and me. Friday and Saturday came and went, and Nick wanted to think about it more.

On Sunday, Nick had to go back to Madison, so when Nick got up that morning Mary said to him that before he leaves, she wanted him to make a decision. Mary can be very persuasive, and all of our kids know that when Mary says something like this, it is time to answer. Well, Nick did wait until he was ready to leave but said he had made a decision and said which agent he wanted, and that agent was the top one on my list. I was ecstatic that he'd selected the one I thought would be the best, a great choice.

I looked at Mary and I could tell she was a little disappointed. I knew right then I would have to say something, so very politely, I said, "Mary, I just want you to know that if Nick had not picked the agent I thought best, I would now be telling Nick why I thought my choice was the best. This is your one chance to do just that, if you would like; otherwise this is the person he

Senior Year in College

chose." Well that was a little blunt, but I knew it had to be said. Mary said it was Nick's choice and she did not want to do that.

Mary and I now knew that Nick had made one of the biggest decisions of his life, and all we could hope was it was the right choice. We told Nick that he had time to think about it because you cannot let them know until after Nick was done playing college ball, which for Nick was after the Bowl game on January 1. However, Nick never wavered from his decision. We had seen our son grow up to be a man, and we were very proud of all of his accomplishments and the decisions he had made in his life.

Some of you may have seen the movie *Jerry McGuire*, which is about a football agent. Well that is one of my favorite movies, but it is not real life, especially for our son. The agent does a lot, and the relationship is so important, but it is not all like the movie. Mary and I had to negotiate many things with the agent for Nick, and we loved the process. However, we were only able to get Nick such a great deal because of our time with the parent who had a son go into the NFL a year before us. I went through the process with the father, who taught me what to expect. The information I received from the father was incredible, and without it who knows what we finally would have negotiated with the agent. All I can say is at the end of the day, we were happy, and Nick was happy with the agent he selected.

The bowl game was upon us and again we took advantage of our time in Florida before the game. Just like high school, this was our last game we would see our son play in college. We were receiving information about where Nick could land in the draft; however, that can go up or down depending how Nick performs on the field, even in this last bowl game. I had repeated this so many times to Nick in his career, but again this was his biggest game thus far because it could help him move up the draft (or down the draft). Well, Nick had a very good game in the bowl game, and we were so proud of him. It was bittersweet because we had made so many friends with the parents and players and now it is over in college. We went to so many tailgates and had so many great times that you do not ever want it to end, but for us, there was possibly a new beginning.

WHAT A RIDE

You cannot sign with an agent until after the player's last game. The agent Nick wanted said he was going to be at the game and asked if he could meet with us after the game. We made arrangements and before we went out to celebrate the game, we did meet with the agent. We had known for over a month this was who Nick wanted, but we could not let the agent know until after the game. We met with the agent, finalized everything, and Nick told him he was his person. Nick was able to sign the papers that day and now it was going to be a very new experience for him and all of us, too.

We had received some good news: that Nick was going to the senior All-Star game. He was invited to the East–West Shrine game that would be played in Houston, Texas. Nick was an alternate for the senior bowl, which is the top bowl for seniors who are going to the pros. Because there were two weeks before this bowl game, the agent took Nick to a facility in Florida for a week to work out. Nick worked out with a former NFL defensive tackle who worked with him the entire week on his technique and conditioning.

It was amazing. There was no down time for Nick. It wasn't any different from when he graduated from high school on a Sunday and then going up to Madison the next day to work out and get prepared to play football in college. Now he was doing the same thing after college, preparing to be drafted into the NFL. My friend who came to all of the high school and college games said he would love to join us at the East–West Shrine game in Houston.

We were very excited and again spent some time in Houston before going to the game. My wife and I had traveled to all the games in college and wanted to continue to travel if our son made it to the next level. There is an expense to this, but I will tell you it is all worth it and we are so glad we took advantage of it.

I know I sound like a broken record, but two weeks later I was telling Nick again this was his biggest game ever. Nick had a good week in practice and was a starter in the game in front

Senior Year in College

of the other defensive tackles. He had just completed starting in college for three years without ever being injured or missing a game and now he was starting in the East–West Shrine game. We had talked to the coaches during the week and heard that Nick had a great week of practice, and they reinforced how important it was for him to have a good game to help him move up in the draft. One of the things parents always worry about is the injuries that can occur. We were no different and it was always on our minds, but at the senior bowl, it was worse because you know if your son is injured it is most likely all over for him. I can say that of all the games, I was happiest for this game to be over and for Nick to finish the bowl game injury-free.

Nick had a very good game with no injuries, and we were told he would most likely be drafted in the third or fourth round, which was up from previous predictions that it would be the fifth or sixth round. It is amazing how this information is known and how much all these scouts know about your son and all the football players who have a chance to play at the next level. Nick truly helped his stock in both bowl games.

We also made a family decision to have Nick go back to Wisconsin and continue taking classes as he prepared for the draft. I know some players take off that semester and only concentrate on football, but we wanted Nick to continue to take classes toward his degree as well as work out and prepare for the draft. I guess our thought process was that he had done it for three and a half years, so he should be able to do it for this semester, too, and because he was still under scholarship. I am still not sure this was what Nick wanted, but he did it.

One of his classes was an independent study, and his topic was what he would financially do if he made it to the NFL. I have to admit, I wrote his paper for him in that class. I was a financial advisor for several years and did write a financial plan for him. I enjoyed the heck out of doing it, and he got an A on that paper. The rest Nick had to do on his own, and he did receive twelve credits that semester with everything else that

What a Ride

was going on his life. The agent helped with so many things, and Nick was eating much healthier and was getting deep tissue massages on a regular basis and was able to work out in the Wisconsin football facilities.

Nick was invited to the NFL Combine that was held at the Indianapolis Colts stadium in Indianapolis. This was another great honor and another possibility to improve his draft pick. Nick worked hard to prepare for the combine. My wife and I wanted to go, and Nick's agent informed us that no spectators were allowed inside the stadium field, only NFL coaches and personnel. His agent said we would not be able to see Nick much, so it did not make sense to go.

Well Mary and I discussed it and we said we didn't care; we were going to go to just see the atmosphere and experience what most parents never do. Mary and I did go and we had the best time at the event. We spent the entire time at the combine, and the first day we did try to get onto the field. Now there are police and a lot of security all over. You can get into the stadium but not inside the field or any of the rooms, like locker rooms. Those who know my wife know that she does not like to be told she cannot do something. Therefore, we tried to get into the stands in the field. We were stopped, but my wife tried, pleading with the officer that her son was in there and she just wanted to see him perform. Well, as you can guess, that did not happen, but I am glad she tried because I know I would never have done that. So what do you do? We knew we could not see our son, so we went to a bar outside the stadium and watched it on the TV.

Now we did tape the entire combine back home, and we could have stayed home and watched it like all the other parents probably did. But not us; we were now in a bar at 9 a.m. in the morning watching it on TV. I will tell you it was amazing because in the bar there were probably a hundred agents doing exactly what we were doing. We met so many wonderful people, and it was amazing because they were all on their phones talking to their agencies about the players they were representing. Mary and I had so much fun. We were in the bars all day long for four days and enjoyed every bit of it.

Senior Year in College

Nick's agent was right; we did not see Nick that much. We did learn how to time it and would see him in the hallways of the stadium occasionally and we were able to take him out to dinner one night; otherwise we were in the bar watching the entire combine. We also had dinner one night with his agent and it was wonderful because we really got to know him on a personal basis. Nick did very well in the combine. He did have one of the highest reps (lifting 225 pounds) out of all the defensive linemen that year. He had thirty-four, and the highest was thirty-eight reps that year. One of the special things we also learned was that Nick did interview with every NFL team at the combine, and that does not always happen. We were feeling good that something special was going to happen for our son. I do remember also every time Nick came on TV, my wife would yell in the bar, stating, "That is my son," and you could tell how proud she was. Knowing now that many parents do not attend, I would highly recommend to any parent who has the chance to go to the combine to watch their son participate and do just what we did. We had so much fun those four days, and we were living the dream.

The information we received after the combine from Nick's agent is that Nick did a good job and it did not hurt him with the activities, and it was another way to get his name out to the NFL teams, especially with the interviews. Nick is a personable person with some good speaking skills, and we and his agent knew this would be a plus for Nick.

The nice thing is that those athletes who attended the combine do get another chance to improve their scores in another event, because some colleges host a Pro Day, and Wisconsin was one of them. The secret is to participate in only those events you want to see an improvement in. The two events in which Nick wanted to improve were his vertical jump and his 40 time. Parents can attend, and we did just that. We met several athletes from different schools in the state that were selected to participate. This was very similar to watching Nick practice in college and was really the last time we were going to

WHAT A RIDE

see the coaches and staff at Wisconsin. Nick did improve both his vertical and 40-yard dash during this event, and he and his agent were very happy that he'd participated in the two events with improvements. We enjoyed being at the event and seeing some of the NFL scouts who attended. Now all we had to do was wait for the NFL draft in April.

Mary and I wanted to do something special for Nick, so we decided we would throw a draft party. The year Nick was drafted, the draft occurred on a weekend. On Saturday was the draft for the first and second rounds, and Sunday was the draft for the third through seventh rounds. Because Nick was projected to go in the third or fourth round, we decided to have the draft party on Sunday.

Mary and I visited many local bars to see which venue would suit our style. We had narrowed it down to three locations. We decided to have it in Hartland, because that was the town Nick played high school football in and was close to our home. We invited all family and friends and had probably invited at least two hundred people. We made all the food and beer arrangements with the bar owner, and he was so excited to host the event. He shut the bar down just for us on Sunday. The draft started at 8 a.m., and we arrived at 7:30 a.m. By 8, the bar was packed with family and friends. To our surprise there were even community people coming who had heard about it and wanted to be part of the action. Mary and I decided that we were not going to stop anyone from coming and felt privileged that they wanted to be part of the special event for our son.

We probably had over three hundred people come and go that day. Everyone started drinking right away in the morning and it was a party. All the TVs were on, and everyone was watching the draft unfold live, drinking, eating, and socializing, not knowing when (or if) Nick's name would be called. The third round came and went, and Nick's name had still not been called. Minutes later, Nick's phone rang, and it is so funny; it was as if we were all magnets and got as close as we could to Nick to listen. It was his agent, just checking in.

Senior Year in College

We all went back to drinking, watching the draft on the TVs, and having fun. The fourth round came and went and Nick's name had not been called. For me, this was the worst feeling ever. We were expecting him to be drafted in the third or fourth round, and now that did not happen. I started thinking: *Is this going to happen? Is Nick going to be drafted?* You want to keep a positive outlook, knowing there are still three more rounds, but there was never a guarantee that he would be drafted or ever play in the NFL. The fifth round started, and Nick received another call. Because it was so loud, Nick started walking to the men's bathroom and went inside to take the phone call. I walked in with him and it was again his agent giving him some words of encouragement.

We went back to the party, the fifth round came and went, and Nick's name was not called. You could now tell that the party was not as lively. Now, our family and friends were not leaving the bar, but the mood had surely changed. Nick was now sitting at the bar and you could see it in his face. I felt so sorry for him and really did not know what to say to him. We just kept waiting and now hoping his name would be called.

It was in the beginning of the sixth round when Nick gets a phone call again. He goes into the men's bathroom and I follow. This time it was his position coach for the first two years in college who was now the defensive line coach for the Washington Redskins. My first reaction was the Washington Redskins were drafting him right now. Well his previous coach says to him, if he is not selected in the sixth round, the Redskins were going to select him with their pick in the seventh round. That was a relief; at least now we knew he was going to be drafted even if it was a later round, and he may reunite with his old position coach whom Nick adored.

We went back out in the bar and everyone wanted to know what had happened. Nick told them, and you could now see the mood change again, and it got loud. No more than ten minutes after that call, Nick got another call and again he headed to the bathroom. This time, not only me but Mary, our kids, and

WHAT A RIDE

even Mary's mom came in. Nick answered the phone and was listening to the person on the other end, and all of a sudden, Nick said, "Yes, I want to be a Carolina Panther."

We now knew he was just drafted. Nick had been talking to John Fox, the head coach of the Carolina Panthers. We all were ecstatic for Nick and hugging him. He continued to talk and finally hung up the phone. Then we heard the biggest roar outside the bathroom. It had just been announced on the TV that the Carolina Panthers had selected Nick as the 181st pick of the draft. Channel 6, our local news channel, was there with a reporter and cameraman. They started to interview Nick, and then they interviewed my wife and me. The one thing that stood out is when Mary was interviewed and commented, "I am so excited I could puke."

Now you know Mary was so happy, but that was not probably the best thing to say, but who cares. Our son was just drafted into the NFL. The funny thing, we learned later, was that the girl Nick was dating at the time had a relative who had bought a few dozen baseball caps that represented every NFL team, and to our surprise he put the Carolina cap on Nick's head when Nick came out of the bathroom. I do know that the rest of the hats were returned to the store after the event.

To this day, we do not know who called the news station or how they knew where we were, but you could not have scripted the scene any better for TV. You have a young kid just get drafted coming out of the men's bathroom in a bar with someone putting a Carolina hat on his head and the news is filming it all. It was a dream come true for my son and for us.

Well, let me tell you, we'd been there since 7:30 a.m., it was now 2:30 p.m., and now it was a real party. We celebrated so much after that and had so much fun, it was unbelievable. Someone started passing out alcohol shots, calling them Panther Piss, and I know I had a lot of Panther Piss that night. Everyone was enjoying the party and celebrating hard. At around 6 p.m. we did pay our bill, and many people in attendance began to leave.

Senior Year in College

It was a long and a very exciting day. However, we were not done. My family and some close friends decided to go to another bar that was on our "top three" list and continued celebrating. We walked into the bar and the bar owner was so glad that we came in. We partied there for several hours. One of my friends thought it would be funny to pull down my pants. He tried to pull down my pants, but the pant leg ripped off, and now I had one pant leg on and my other leg was exposed. All I remember was that the bar owner came around and grabbed the pant leg that was ripped off. I thought he was going to throw it away. We continued to celebrate until around midnight. This was a night I never wanted to end. We were having so much fun.

We did finally decide to go home, and one of the most memorable parts of the entire day was when we got home. It was our entire family—my wife, Nick, my younger son Alex, my daughter Abbey, and me. We all sat down in the family room and started to reflect on the day. All of us were telling stories of the event; we had taped the news segment and watched that again. It was so nice and really was such a private family moment that I have never forgotten it to this day.

One ending to this wonderful story is about the pant leg that was ripped off my leg in the bar. About two weeks after Nick was drafted, my wife and I went back to that bar for dinner. We walked in the door and the bar owner saw us and said, "Just wait a minute." He went in the back room and came out with a ladder. He sets the ladder up by the entrance of the bar and starts to climb the ladder. I look up, and there was my pant leg stapled to the ceiling. He pulls the pant leg down and says to me, "This pant leg is making me money." He asks me to write something on the pant leg, and so I write, "One of the best days of my life, my son Nick Hayden made it to the pros!" I signed and dated the pant leg. The bar owner said, "This is great," and proceeded to staple the pant leg back up on the ceiling near the front entrance.

It has been over eleven years now, and that pant leg is still on the ceiling. Occasionally, I will receive a text from someone I

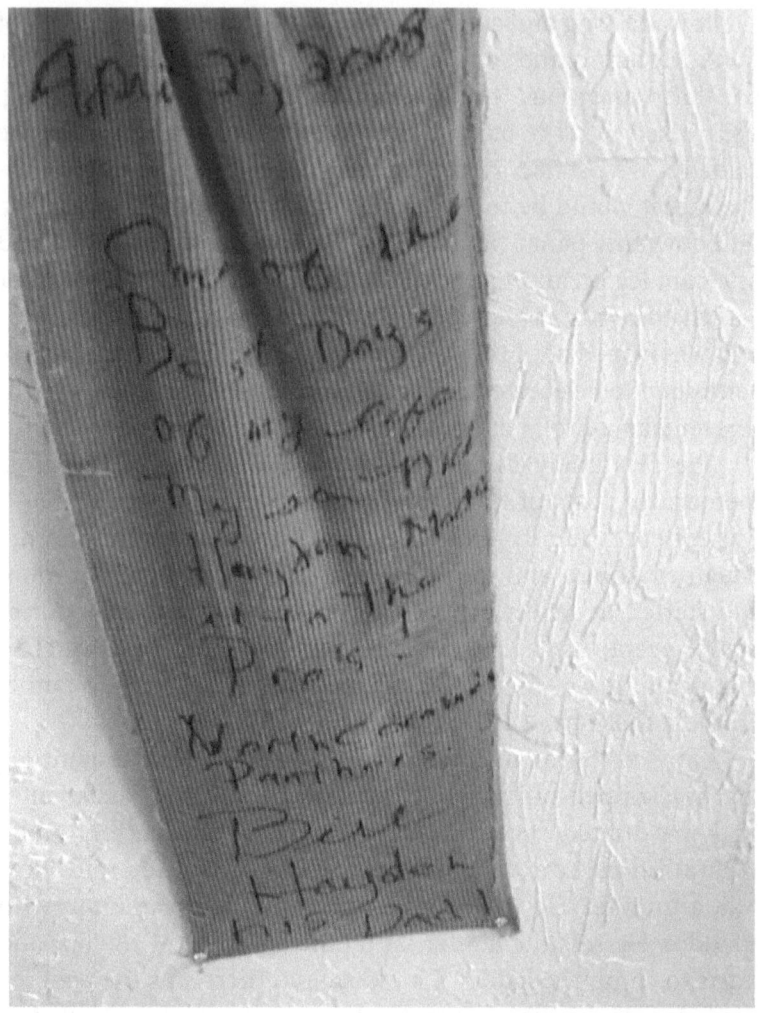

Author Bill Hayden's pant leg, still hanging in the Ox and Cat's bar in Merton, WI

know with a picture of the pant leg still hanging from the ceiling in the bar. I am not sure how much money that pant leg made for the bar owner, but I was happy to help his business out in some small way, and it is such a great memory.

As you read you can tell that my wife and I have taken advantage of everything we possibly could with all the events my son has gone through. It is kind of funny because we were

Senior Year in College

really having fun through my son, who had to put in all of the hard work to get where he is, and we were truly enjoying the ride. He is my son, and I may be a little biased, but you do not get to the pros without a lot of hard work, dedication, learning, skill, avoiding injuries, and a little luck. My son had now done something that most kids can only dream about, and now that dream had come true.

Now more than ever, he had to prove himself over again if he wanted to play in the NFL. He just was drafted in the sixth round. He was not a high draft choice, did not go in the round that was expected, and was on a team that never was even on his radar when he went through the entire NFL process. This was our first lesson. You can hear information from agents, scouts, sports writers, et cetera, but it is truly only information, and nearly none of it was accurate, and it is not real until it happens.

We just experienced this and never forgot it because as our son played in the NFL, this similar scenario happened to Nick many different times. We now have so many memories from high school and college football and did not know what would happen next. All we could do was wait and watch what would happen, knowing the wonderful ride could be over at any time.

CHAPTER 6

Nick's First NFL Team Carolina Panthers

As soon as Nick was drafted, he started getting information from the Carolina Panthers. He would have to report to rookie camp in a week, so there was not much downtime again for him. We were so excited for him, and Nick was very excited, too. Once he was in rookie camp, we started watching everything online for the Carolina Panthers. There was not a thing my wife and I would miss. Every night we would call him to find out how practice went and how he was doing. I just remember calling him right from the start and always asking if he was injured.

I know it sounds funny, but even though we worried about injuries during his high school and college years, it does become different in the pros. You know that just one injury and it could be over, especially for a player who was not drafted high. Every day we would ask him so many questions, and I know Nick did not like all the questions, but he always answered them to keep us informed.

At the end of rookie camp, which is a long weekend, Nick said he felt he did well. On the Carolina website, there were some reports that Nick did well, so it was good to hear. Nick came home after the camp and spent some time with us, and it really was the first time in while we got to spend some quality time with Nick. One of the things we did have to do was find a

Nick's First NFL Team

financial advisor for Nick. Now that he had an agent, his agent gave us several names. This was very nice because when we were looking for the agent, we basically started at square one. Now we had someone my son trusted to give us advice.

We contacted each one and discussed the financials for Nick. Nick decided on one that he thought would be a good fit and he came out to visit with us. Just like the agents, they do go through how they will help your son and some of their ways they will invest the money. I was a financial advisor at one point in my career, so I knew what to ask and what to look for, which helped tremendously. When we met with the financial advisor, there was one interesting story that I recall. He started asking Mary and me questions about ourselves. One of the things we told him was that we were planning to retire in about twelve years. The financial advisor made a comment and said, "Wouldn't it be neat if Nick retired from the NFL the same time you two did?"

I have to admit, I started laughing out loud because here is a kid who just got drafted and in a late round and we still did not know if he would make the team or ever play a down in the NFL. For those who may not have heard the phrase before, NFL stands for "Not for Long." In addition, the average career length in the NFL is three years, and it was just funny that he had said that. I think both Mary and I are so realistic, so as nice as that sounded and though his intentions were sincere, the chances were slim of that occurring.

Now Nick went into training camp in the spring. He was working hard and getting adjusted to the NFL. I asked him one day what the difference was in the NFL compared with college. Nick said matter-of-factly, "Every player is good now, and the main difference is that every player is bigger, stronger, and faster."

This only makes sense when you think about it; there are many high school football players, then the number of players who make it to a Division 1 program diminishes drastically, and then the percentage is so much smaller of those athletes who

Nick, #78, playing during his Rookie year against the New Orleans Saints

get to the NFL. On another occasion, I asked Nick what was different with the practices in the NFL. Again, Nick said matter-of-factly, "Dad, we are doing the same thing I did in peewee league, in high school and in college. I take the same step, we do the same drills, and I work on my technique, lift, and stretch the same. The difference is everyone is bigger, stronger, and faster."

NICK'S FIRST NFL TEAM

What I learned that day is that the fundamentals do not change at every level; the basics are so important, and the only difference truly is that the players are bigger, stronger, faster, and they are all great athletes. I stopped asking him that question after that. Maybe I got the answer or understood that much better, but it was interesting because I had taught my son so many things about football, and now my son was starting to teach me about football.

This also brings me to a good point with transitioning to learning from my son. When Nick was in college, many people would ask me if I was living through my son as he played college football. I was always taken back at that and would say, "No, I played through college and had a great football career. I understand the game and I am not living through my son."

I truly meant what I said. However, when Nick got to the pros, I may not have realized it at first, but I was now living through my son's experiences and understand that it is because I never made it to the NFL. If I were asked that same question now, I would proudly say, "Yes, I am living through my son and enjoying every minute of it." I can say that not many people get to play NFL football and then have a son play in the NFL, so I was going to live through his experiences.

Nick now signed his contract with the Carolina Panthers, which was a four-year deal. His agent negotiated it for him, and Nick received a signing bonus in the appropriate amount when he was drafted. I still remember he wanted to buy a car with some of his signing bonus. Nick wanted a Cadillac and it was a little pricey, knowing that he was just starting his career. We talked to Nick and he finally decided to buy a Chrysler 300 Touring Sedan. It was half of what the Cadillac would have cost, and we were happy that he just made a great financial decision with buying a car.

I can say Nick did make many good financial decisions throughout his career, and we are very proud of him for that. As you know and hear in the news, many football players do not make good financial decisions, and many leave with next to

WHAT A RIDE

nothing when their football career is done. Nick also kept that Chrysler throughout his football career, and it was not until after he retired that he bought himself that Cadillac.

Nick went through the mini-camps, training camps, and then to the preseason camp. These new experiences were so exciting. Because we still did not know whether our son was going to make the team, we decided to go to two preseason games at Carolina his rookie year. Now we are in the Carolina stadium for the first time. Our seats are in the first section in the end zone. Not bad seats. I can still remember Nick going out on the field during the preseason game. It was so exciting. We had watched Nick play so many games already, but having him on that field and being in the NFL was the highlight of our life at that time. Mary and I also loved Carolina and really liked Charlotte. We were in heaven. Nick played in all the preseason games and had what I thought was a good preseason at Carolina. He made it through the first two cuts, which is very nerve-racking because you wait in your room and hope that you don't get a call. Can you imagine how hard it is for a twenty-one-year-old man to wait to see if you get a phone call to let you know to come to the office and hear you didn't make the team?

Now that it was the final cuts, the time came to find out if he made the team or not. Nick did get a phone call and he did not make the team. Now can you imagine what goes through your head? Fortunately, for Nick, the coach told him they were going to sign him to the practice squad the next day. I was extremely sad, probably even depressed, and so many thoughts went through my head. The biggest thing we learned very quickly is that a contract does not mean anything. In all honesty, it is an invitation to try out for an NFL team. You must make the team first before the contract is fulfilled. Nick's contract was declared invalid, and Nick's agent had to renegotiate a one-year practice squad contract.

We were happy that they still wanted Nick and that there was still a chance he could play football in the NFL. Just think of how many players go home and hope another team wants

Nick's First NFL Team

them. This is either the last time they play football or they just wait for a team to call them up. We also learned from Nick that he'd played through the preseason games with an old shoulder injury and didn't want to go to the training staff to let them know because he was afraid he would have gotten cut, which he now realized was dumb. Nick told them about it after he got on the practice squad, got an MRI, and ended up getting a shot, which helped tremendously.

We now were learning a lot of what goes on in the NFL that most people do not realize. Nick was very happy that he was still on the team even if it was the practice squad. The coaches said they were still high on Nick, and the competition is so fierce that these are some of the consequences. Mary and I were glad that we'd gone to the preseason games because it could have been the last time we saw our son play in an NFL game.

Another interesting story occurred when Nick was a rookie. Mary and I went to a preseason game at Carolina. We went out to the bars with Nick one night, and I say to the bartender as a proud parent, "Hey, this is Nick Hayden from the Carolina Panthers." The bartender perked up and, all of a sudden, Nick looks at me and says, "Knock it off, Dad." Well I laughed it off and did not think much of it, and we had a fun night.

The next night, we go out to dinner and I again say to the server, "Hey, this is Nick Hayden from the Carolina Panthers." The server gets very big eyes and smiles, asks a couple questions, and then walks away. Nick now looks at me and, for the first time in my life, I was scolded by my son. Nick says, "Dad I told you yesterday to knock it off; now you did it again. I want to be able to go out in this town and have no one know who I am. Please do not do it again."

It was such a learning experience for me. I was so used to teaching others, and now I'd learned a very valuable lesson from my son: how important it was to him not to be recognized, so he could just live a normal life when he went out. And I learned how humble Nick really was. I knew Nick was a humble kid, but I guess a light bulb finally went on in my head to really understand this. Besides talking to family and friends about Nick and the NFL, we never went out and brought that up as I had in those two situations. Well, maybe once or twice after that, when I was drinking, but it was not often. I can say that to this day and through his football career, I truly have an appreciation for this now, because we have been able to go out with Nick in many public places and not have the publicity of an NFL player, and we were able to be a normal family. It is something I now cherish, and I appreciate my son for scolding me that day.

Nick continued to be on the practice squad that year. Carolina was having a very good season. This will sound terrible, but what you learn is that the only way Nick could be moved back up on the team is if someone in his position would be injured and cannot play. This was our first experience with something like this, and I am not saying you hope someone is injured, but you do start watching games to see if there is an injury at his position as a defensive tackle. The other thing you learn very quickly is that another team could pick up your son from the practice squad if a person in his position is injured from that team. It is really a completely different experience when you begin to learn about the NFL and how it operates.

Week after week, you wait to see if there will be a change. Suddenly, Nick calls us with two games remaining in his rookie season and says that one of the defensive tackles is injured and he may get pulled up to the regular team from the practice squad. My heart was racing with excitement and I started asking a million questions. Nick said he would know by tomorrow. That night, all I can remember is praying that he is called up.

The next day he called and said he is going to be activated for the game. Now he has to go through another contract for the rest of the season. This is now his third contract that year. Because it was the night before the game, we were not able to get plane tickets for that game, so we did stay home and had a huge party to watch the game. It was so exciting because of what all happened to Nick and now, hopefully, he gets his chance to play in his first NFL regular season game. Nick did not start but

Nick's First NFL Team

he did get in the game for several series and got a tackle. I have to say I've seen my son make so many tackles in his career, but that first tackle in the NFL was awesome. Because we had been to almost every game live in his career, it was really no different watching on TV, except I know I was more animated and was very excited.

So after that first game, we tried to find out if Nick would be playing in the next game or not. He did not know if the injured player would be back or not, so it was a day-by-day situation. We did not know if we should buy tickets or not and finally decided that we would not, and if they won this game, Carolina would be in the playoffs and we would go to that game. Again, it was a last-minute decision for that game, but Nick did play again in the last regular season game and again did really well, and they won. Mary and I got plane tickets, Nick got tickets for us to the game, and now we were buying more Carolina wear and were very excited to go to the playoff game.

Even though we had been there during the preseason games, now that Nick was playing on the team in his rookie season with the team making the playoffs, it was so exciting. The Panther Stadium was packed and the crowd was wild. It was unbelievable. Nick did not start but did play in several series in the first half. Another defensive tackle was injured, and in the second half Nick came out playing in the first series. This was another big moment for Nick that would, hopefully, help him make the team in the next year. Unfortunately, the team lost and the season was all over.

Now the contract Nick received was only good for that year. Well, we learned in a couple of days they were bringing Nick back on the team but only extended a one-year contract. Now we were learning about the NFL and how it works, and it was nothing like we thought. We were still very happy that our son had another opportunity to try out again. Because that is truly what a contract is: an invitation to try out for the team. Until you make the team, the contract does not mean a whole heck of a lot.

WHAT A RIDE

Nick had decided to live in Carolina and to do his off-season workouts there. Nick got a trainer in the area. Another thing that happened was, because I am the dad, I told Nick there was no down time after his rookie season and kind of made him start working out right away, because as I told him, he needed to be ready to make the team the next season. Nick did it, and I learned another valuable lesson. When the camps came around, Nick was extremely tired because he'd never let his body recover after the season. This was my mistake, and Nick let me know that if he continued to play football after this season he was going to let his body recover properly.

Nick did do just that through the rest of his career, and I now understood the impact that the game and practices put on your body in the NFL. I can say from that time after his rookie year, I kept my mouth shut and let my son make the choices; he knew what was best for him. This was another example of the transition for me from being the father.

One of the things Nick asked me to do early on in his career was to help him with his agent. I was very involved and would be the one asking the agent all the questions. Nick had given me his NFL player's contract that all football players get, and it is over two hundred pages long. I had read that book three times through and had a good handle on what players got and so forth. That season there were some questions about whether Nick would be credited for the season or not, with playing the three games. After some research from his agent, Nick was credited for the season, and that was a big plus for him after all that had just happened in his rookie year.

My wife and I were still very busy with daughter Abbey, who now was playing freshman and select basketball. We went from football right into having basketball tournaments every weekend. We loved it and there is nothing better than watching your kids participate in an activity and especially sports. This was our life now for almost fifteen years, and we enjoyed every minute of it with all of our kids.

Nick's First NFL Team

Abbey in her freshman year of basketball at Arrowhead

Something else special happened after Nick's rookie season. Nick reconnected with someone he knew in grade school. Her name was Milania, and Mary and I did not know Milania back in grade school because she did not go to the same school but would hang out with Nick and his friends after school because she lived in the neighborhood. Milania was finishing her college degree in Arizona, and Nick went to visit Milania in the off-season. Milania came out to visit Nick, and that April before the next season Milania came out to live with Nick in Carolina. It was the start of a long relationship; we got to know Milania very well, and eventually they got married.

Nick participated in the off-season workouts, mini-camps and finally the preseason camp. We decided to go to two-preseason games again that year because we now learned it was the right thing to do just in case Nick did not make the team. Nick was playing very well now and had a very good preseason. This time it turned out better; he did not get the call that lets you know you did not make the team. I can still remember we were all waiting to see if Nick would get this call. After a certain hour, if you do not hear anything it means you made the team. How nerve-racking for every player trying out for the team. This year Nick was now on the team. Nick did start a couple games that year and was part of the defensive tackle rotation.

Mary and I now started to plot out what games we wanted to attend that year. We selected several games in Carolina and then those games that he would play in the Midwest that were within driving distance from our home in Wisconsin. Mary and I really liked the Carolina area and were enjoying the games. One of the things that Nick did for us throughout his career was get us tickets to the games. Nick always got two free tickets to the game, but now that Milania was in his life, he had to purchase an extra ticket when we came to the games. Mary and I paid our way to get to the stadium and paid for the hotel for away games, but Nick always bought the extra ticket for the games. It was his way of showing us his appreciation for what we all had done for him.

Nick's second season was so exciting. He was fitting in very well with the team and was starting to really contribute at his position. One of the hardest things for us to believe was that our son, who was always a good football player, was now playing

Nick's First NFL Team

alongside some great football players. One, whom most people know, was defensive end Julius Peppers. It was so humbling that our son was part of players like that. Nick started a couple games in his second season because of injuries to other defensive tackles, but really was the rotation man that year.

The nice thing about playing on the defensive side as a lineman is that you do play a lot in the game because, basically, every other series you go in to keep the players fresh. If Nick had been an offensive lineman, that would not always have been the case. Most starters play the game unless there's an injury. Therefore, you may not ever know if you were going to get in on the offensive side until an injury occurred. This was nice for us because Nick was contributing to the team every game.

Nick's second year in the pros was so good for him. You could see how Nick was progressing, getting better every week. He started to feel very comfortable, especially with the speed of the game. That year the Carolina Panthers did not make the playoffs. Nick did receive another one-year contract with the team at the end of the season. This is how it works for someone like Nick. He had a good season and still was not a starter, but he did contribute very nicely with the team. We were very excited that Nick was going to play again with the Carolina Panthers, and we could tell it was a good fit for him. Nick got along with coaches, his teammates, and was jelling on the team.

In Nick's third year in the NFL, he again made the team. He was not a starter yet, but you could see he was being groomed. This was Nick's biggest year thus far. The team was looking for someone to step up at defensive tackle. The team started to bring other defensive tackles in to try out. This was a very interesting time because we started noticing these things, and many things go through your mind. The interesting thing is that these players came and went, and in the fourth game of the season, Nick was named the starter for the first time, not because of an injury, but because he'd earned it. Of all the things we've seen our son do throughout his football career, this was the biggest moment for us. Our son was going to be a true

WHAT A RIDE

starter in the NFL as a defensive tackle. This was an away game with the St. Louis Rams. We did something a little different this game. Not sure if it was the right thing to do at the time, but Nick asked us if we wanted tickets for the game. Mary and I knew we were going to the game, but we told Nick no, we were going to watch it on TV. We did this because usually the away tickets are not very good seats, and we wanted to buy good seats right behind the visitors' bench. I wanted to buy them online, but Mary said let's go there and scalp the tickets. Mary thought we had a better chance of getting great seats for a better price. I was a little skeptical but went along with Mary's suggestion. It was not that easy, but Mary was right.

We started looking for tickets early that morning and found great tickets behind the visitors' bench for a very good price. Now Nick thought we were going to watch the game on TV and had no idea we were coming. We wanted to surprise him as he came out of the tunnel before the game. We had done this at the Carolina games and had got down to the tunnel many times to say hi to Nick from the stands at the tunnel. Therefore, we got into the game early and went over to where the Carolina Panthers would come out. This was on the opposite side of the visitors' bench.

We started to work our way to the tunnel from the stands. We almost got there when a security guard stopped us and said we cannot go down there because we do not have tickets to that section. Well, Mary goes on to explain to the security guard that he doesn't understand, that we have a son who plays for the Carolina Panthers, and this is his first official start in the NFL and we want to say good luck to him and let him know we are at the game. Well the security guard says to Mary, "*You* do not understand; your tickets are not for this section, and you cannot go down there."

Our hearts dropped. Here we were going to surprise our son, and now he was not even going to know we were at the game. All of a sudden, a couple who were St. Louis fans had heard us and said to the security guard, "Hey, if we give them our tickets until the team comes out of the tunnel and we stay in the corridor, can they then see their son?" The security guard said, "Yeah, that'll work," and this wonderful couple gave us their tickets.

Mary and I hurried to the front of the tunnel. We were in the first row about ten feet up from the field. All of a sudden, the defense came to the end of the tunnel. There was Nick right in front. We yelled down to him and he looked up. He had no idea we were coming, and all of sudden he sees his parents at the tunnel before he runs out. He had a smile from ear to ear, and you could tell how excited he was to see us. Both Mary and I said some words to him, and then we both said we loved him, and then several of the players looked at us and start laughing. I guess we forgot that these are grown men and how many parents can say they just told their son they loved him at the end of the tunnel before they ran onto the field. Well we just did it.

We thanked the couple for what they did, bought them a beer, and proceeded to our seats. We were in the twelfth row. Excellent seats, but not close enough to the bench where Nick could hear us yelling at him the entire game that we were behind him.

One of the most interesting things was that Nick continued to look for us in the area where the tunnel was, but we had never told him we had seats behind the bench. It made me realize how important it is to our kids, and to kids of any parent, to know that Mom and Dad are there watching them, no matter what activity it may be. I am sure Nick was a little disappointed when we told him we were not coming to the game during the week, but once we surprised him at the tunnel, it was all worth it. Nick went on to have a phenomenal game for his first official start in the NFL because he earned it. What a ride.

The interesting thing about life is that we were on top of the world. We had a son who was now a legitimate starter in the NFL. However, we had to deal with just the opposite. Our daughter Abbey was involved with sports for years and was now a sophomore in high school and trying out for the volleyball team. All the children and my wife, Mary, were good volleyball players. Abbey tried out and we awaited the answer and found out Abbey did not make the team. It was devastating to Abbey and to us. We were now on both sides of the spectrum with sports.

As any parent who goes through this will tell you, your heart goes out for your child. You wonder why this would happen, but competition in any sport can be brutal, and now we have to keep our daughter's ego and head up. We did just that and told her she still has basketball and to continue to work hard and get ready for basketball. Abbey does just that; she works hard preparing for basketball tryouts. The time comes for basketball tryouts and she goes through them. We asked Abbey how she did, and she said she felt confident she did well. Finally, she gets the news and she does not make the basketball team as a sophomore.

We now had a daughter who'd been playing basketball since the age of five years old starting at the YMCA through select teams, and she now does not make the team in a second sport as a sophomore. It is devastating to her and to us. What do you say? How do we try to make her feel good about herself? She has two brothers who played their sports through high school and now she does not make the team on two sports as a sophomore. It was a hard couple of weeks, but Abbey did bounce back. She decided to go out for intramural basketball that year, and the team she was on won the intramural basketball league. It was such a great thing to see her continue to play basketball and try to make the best out of a very sad situation. That spring, she came home and said to Mary and me, "I'm going to try out for the tennis team."

We were very happy because it showed she was willing to try new things and not give up. These are characteristics of all of our children, and we are very proud of them. Abbey did make the team and started playing tennis as a sophomore, having never played the sport before. The nice thing is that my wife, Mary, is the true athlete. One of the sports she excelled in was

Nick's First NFL Team

Abbey her senior year at an Arrowhead tennis match

tennis, and I am hoping that trait is something Abbey has, too. Abbey ended up playing tennis through the rest of her high school years, and Mary and I enjoyed watching her play tennis and watching her grow in the sport. We were extremely proud and impressed with Abbey for what she went through and how she overcame disappointment and did not let it hold her back with trying something new and then succeeding in it.

During the time Abbey was going through her sport hardships, we began to go to more football games because Nick was starting. Just as with Abbey, you do not know when this is going to end, so you do want to take advantage of it. Nick rented a house from a player who was traded from Carolina, and it was in a nice community. We would stay with Nick and Milania. The place had a community pool, which was right up our alley. We would come in late on Friday and usually stay until Monday. Nick and Milania would pick us up at the airport. Nick would usually have a morning practice on Saturday and then come home; we could spend the afternoon with him, and then around 5 p.m. he would have to leave to go to the hotel where all the players stayed until the game on Sunday.

We were starting to have some fun before the games now. We would spend time at the pool and met some people from the neighborhood through Milania. We were starting to become popular with the neighbors and we would hang out with them at the pool on Saturdays and even had some pool parties. We always got up early on Sundays and got to the games early to see what was going on around the stadium and would be in the stadium to watch warmups before the game. We were having a lot of fun, and Nick was starting every game and playing well. After the game, we would go out for dinner together and sometimes Nick and I would go out to the bars with some other players. We were truly living the dream.

I took off on Mondays from the company I worked for, but the management meeting was on Mondays. The owner asked that I call in for the management meeting each Monday when I was away. I had no problem doing this because I was kept in the loop and gave my information to the other managers during the meeting. Because of the community pool where Nick lived, I started to go to it early in the morning on Mondays and I saw that no one was in the pool. Therefore, every Monday I would get on a floating device in the pool and get on the phone for the management meeting. Not a bad way to spend two hours while on the phone for the meeting. I was living the dream.

That year we went to Tampa Bay for a game and stayed on the beach. On Monday, I told Mary I had to make my management phone call and she said, "Why don't we walk the beach while you are on the call." Not a bad idea except I forgot to mute my phone as we were walking. All of a sudden, one of the managers back

Nick's First NFL Team

at the office blurts out, "Hey, Bill, is that waves I am hearing in the background?" I was very embarrassed; I did not say a word and immediately muted my phone. We were having a blast and getting work done, too. Not only having our son play football in the NFL and going to the games, which were awesome, but also enjoying ourselves doing so many other activities every weekend. We did not know how long it was going to last and just wanted to take advantage of it. There was also a cost to doing this several times in a season, and now we were starting to save money through a budget for the football season.

It was getting to the end of the season, and Carolina was not having a great year. One of the things I noticed was Nick always had some minor injuries, not enough to keep him out of a game, but a lot of aches and pains. A day before one of the last games that season, I remember Nick getting out of his chair on Saturday afternoon to go to the hotel. He was like an old grandpa getting out of a chair, and I looked at Nick and said, "How are you going to play tomorrow?" Nick just said he would be all right and left.

I thought back to my college days and remembered that on Sundays, after a Saturday game, I was a little sore but always bounced right back. I now realized that this was not college football and that at this level the game is so much more brutal. The sad thing that I remembered after that game we went out had some fun and Nick seemed fine, but the next day when Nick was going to take us to the airport and he got out of his chair, it was ten times worse than an old grandpa. All I could think was, *This is our twenty-three-year-old son, and he is really getting beat up in the game that we all love, including him.* I can say I saw that many other times during Nick's career, and it is something that most people do not realize, how truly physical the game is at the NFL level, unless you see it through your own eyes with your son.

Well, with that said, Nick did start every game the rest of the year and even though the team did not do well, Nick was getting better and had his best year so far in the NFL. The team did not make it to the playoffs, and after the season the head coach was let go and a new coach was hired with many new faces on the coaching staff. Nick only had a one-year contract, so we did not know what was going to happen. Nick was now a legitimate starter and we only hoped they offered him another contract. Well they did give Nick another contract and again it was for one year, and everything looked like it would be good, even with the changes with the head coach and the coaching staff.

We have always been so proud of our kids' accomplishments. I did realize no matter what our kids did we were very blessed to have great children. I was so happy that I had a son who was starting in the NFL, but I can truly say I was more proud for something else than Nick being a starter in the NFL. On Nick's twenty-fourth birthday, which was on February 4, and having played in the NFL for three years, I called him up in Carolina. I said to Nick, "Happy birthday," and then proceeded to give him a fatherly speech. I told Nick that I was so proud of him for playing and being a starter in the NFL, but there was something I was even more proud of him for, and that was that he had never been fined in the NFL, for three years now. For those who don't know, a player can get fined for a lot of things, like arriving late to practice, coming late to a meeting, being overweight or underweight, curfew violations, wearing the wrong piece of uniform, on-the-field infractions, et cetera. I told Nick he had never been fined for anything and asked him how many players could say that. Nick said, "Not many, Dad." I told Nick that is why I am so proud of him, because that is the character and integrity his mom and I tried to instill in him and all of our children, and we were very proud of this even more than being a starter in the NFL.

Now after my speech, I did not know what he would say, and all I got out of him was, "Well, thank you, Dad." I was not sure what I was going to hear, but I can say, this was truly one of the most memorable speeches I gave to my son, and it was so true about his character in the NFL.

Nick's First NFL Team

Another memorable moment that year was when Nick proposed to Milania. Nick is our oldest child, so this was also a new experience for us. We were so excited for him, Milania, and for all of us. It is amazing how fast everything was going, and one thing I always have told younger parents often is really enjoy everything your children do because they do grow up fast and you don't want to miss anything. Mary and I truly lived to this philosophy as our children were growing.

That off-season Nick did take a break from football. I now realize how important it is to let your body rest and recover. Nick went through the mini-camps, training camps, and all required practices and was still the starter on defense. We felt confident that Nick was going to make the team even with the coaching changes and even though Carolina drafted two other defensive tackles. Everything was falling into place. Now the preseason games started and we decide we would only attend one game and would wait for the regular season games to attend. Nick started every preseason game.

We learned something very quickly that year, though. After the fourth and final preseason game as in the past, you wait *not* to hear that phone call, because if you do not get a call after a certain time, you've made the team. This year Nick did get a call, he had to go in, and it was his last day as a Carolina Panther. We never saw it coming and we understood that this is a business, and why they make their decisions we may never know, but it shows you can be on a team thinking you are doing well to find out you are not part of that team anymore. It was devastating to get that call from our son. We felt so bad and so many things go through your head, from *Why did this happen?* to *Is this the last time he ever plays football?*

CHAPTER 7

THE CINCINNATI BENGALS COME CALLING

Well it was a new chapter for us. Nick's agent explained that now Nick must sit and wait to see if anyone else picks him up in the next week. Nick heard nothing from any other team. The next step is you wait for an injury on a team. That is exactly what we did. We learned that there were some teams that had an interest in Nick, so Mary and I started watching NFL football games of those teams which we'd heard had an interest. We began to watch games to see if a defensive tackle was injured on that team.

I remember looking at Mary one day during a game and saying to her, "I cannot believe we are watching football for injuries; this just is not right." However, it is what you do. Week after week went by, and every week you think, *Is his career over?* We did not want it to be over. We were living the dream and we did not want that dream to end.

Finally, at the end of the season, Nick's agent called and said there was interest by the Cincinnati Bengals because a defensive tackle was injured and was out for the rest of the season. So Nick immediately got on a plane and did a workout in front of the coaches and staff. The next day he came back home not knowing if he would get a call or not. The other thing you learn is that Nick was not the only player trying out at that point. There were several defensive tackles, and now he was competing

The Cincinnati Bengals Come Calling

again against others. Well, Nick got great news and was picked up by the Cincinnati Bengals and signed another contract for the remainder of the year.

Nick had to get on a plane that day, make it to practice the next day, and play in the game that Sunday. Wow, we were learning how fast all of this could happen. Now we were Cincinnati fans. One of the things that is so interesting is that growing up in Wisconsin, we were big Green Bay Packer fans, but when you have a son in the NFL, no matter what team they are on, you become a fan of that team. It is amazing how many people have asked me this question. Are you now a Packer fan or at one time a Panther fan and now a Cincinnati fan? It was so hard to fathom, because I would think most parents would become a fan of the team their son was playing on. Yet I was asked that question repeatedly and the answer always was I am a Panther fan and now I am a Cincinnati fan because it is the team my son is on. Nick was a backup on the Bengals but again played in the rotation.

That year the Bengals made it to the playoffs and now this was Nick's second time being part of a playoff series in his career. The Bengals unfortunately lost the game, and the season was over. The nice thing is that they did offer Nick another one-year contract.

It was exciting to know that Nick had another opportunity at continuing his football career. We did not know much about Cincinnati but were excited to learn the team and the city.

Nick again went through the mini-camps, training camps and now you have to start all over. It does not matter if you played in the league for three years you now need to prove yourself again. Nick did extremely well in the camps and he was receiving high praise from the team. It looked very promising that Nick would have a great chance of making the team. Nick would call us and tell us stories about his defensive coordinator. Nick could tell he really liked his work ethic.

One story that sticks out is when Nick told us that in the film room that the defensive coordinator would always say

Nick, #98, playing for Cincinnati against the Atlanta Falcons

during the camps, "Who is that person making those tackles on the field?" Nick said that one of the defensive linemen would say, "It is Nick Hayden," and the defensive coordinator would say, "That's right; look at him making all those tackles."

Nick said this happened several times. Nick knew that the coach was pointing him out because he was the new person on the team. And for Nick to even tell us that story, we knew it meant something because it was always hard to pull information out of Nick.

As we entered into the preseason, Mary and I were back to watching preseason games. It is amazing; you have to start at the beginning again and not knowing if Nick will make the team, and you do want to go to the games just in case he doesn't. That year we went to the first three preseason games. Nick was playing very well and you could tell he was fitting well with the team. The third preseason game was against the Green Bay Packers and us being from Wisconsin our team growing up was the Green Bay Packers. Even though this was a preseason game, it was a big game for us. It is interesting how the news stations know that your son is from Wisconsin and how even

The Cincinnati Bengals Come Calling

in a preseason game, the media from Wisconsin hyped up our son. It was nice to see and hear because we had heard so much from the media when Nick was a Wisconsin Badger, but that does go away when they go play for a team that is not in your state.

The game was probably one of the most memorable games we saw at that time. Nick truly came out to play that day. It was amazing, we were in the stands and every other play you would hear Nick's name over the loudspeaker as getting the tackle on defense. It was unbelievable and never, to this day, did we hear his name as often as we did that day. I was very pumped up because I knew that he had just proven himself and now really had a good chance of making the team. Right after the game I had to go to the bathroom, and I walked into the stadium bathroom and the radio announcers were talking about the game, about Nick Hayden being the best player on the field that day. It was such a motivating thing to hear, and when I came out, my wife said, "What were you yelling about in the bathroom?"

I'd been so excited when I heard them say that he was the best player on the field, and I began yelling and never realized how loud I was. We went out that night and celebrated pretty hard because of all that had just happened. A friend who lived in our hometown called me the next day. He'd gone to the Cincinnati game and I didn't even know it. He said he'd gone with a client and then he congratulated me on the game. My friend said that right after the game, he went out to eat with the client, and on the way back to his hotel room, about 9 p.m., he turned on the radio to see what they were saying about the game, and he could not believe it. The radio announcers were still talking about Nick and the game he'd had. That was special and what a ride we were on.

The next week Nick was practicing and preparing for the final preseason game. During one play, Nick received a leg injury. It was bad enough to keep him out of practice. When I heard this, my heart dropped. Here Nick was doing so well, just

WHAT A RIDE

had probably one of his best games ever, and now he was injured. It was his (and our) biggest nightmare. Now what happens? Do they see enough in Nick to keep him and sign him to the fifty-three-man roster? Do they let him go now? We are now learning how fast things can change, and we had already seen so many different things happen to our son in the NFL. The game can be so frustrating not only for the player but for the parents as well. Nick did get the bad news, and they waived him. He did receive a buyout and would have to be inactive for the first four games of the season because of the buyout. These are the important reasons why you have an agent—to help make some decisions for the players. This decision was a critical one, and Nick made the decision to take the buyout because now he had four credited years in the NFL, so he now would be invested in the NFL pension plan. I look at all the decisions I have made in my life, and my son was making more important decisions in his twenties than I had at that age. More important, does Nick ever play in the NFL again because of this decision? Our son had to look at his future and make that decision, compared with playing again in the NFL. It is amazing how many decisions our young son was making in his life, but he made many good decisions.

So here we were, after the fourth game of the season, and we were watching football games looking for defensive tackles to get injured, hoping our son gets another shot at the NFL. Game after game, week after week, Nick does not hear anything. The chances appear to get slimmer and slimmer. No one is calling. *Is this the end?* Do we now just have great memories of all the good years we had? The season was over, and no team had called Nick. I have to admit I thought it was over, but I can say up to that point that Mary and I took every opportunity through Nick's career to watch him play and enjoyed every minute of it.

As quickly as we were thinking it was over, Nick got a phone call from the Dallas Cowboys, and they wanted to work him out for the next season. Nick got on a plane and headed to Dallas. They worked out Nick, and he comes back home. We

The Cincinnati Bengals Come Calling

are all asking Nick how it went, and Nick said he thought he did well. One of the things I admire about Nick is he's always level headed and may say something like he feels he did well, but never would he jump the gun. He would always say things like, "We will have to wait until it happens." And nothing happens until they offer him a contract and he signs it. Well, a few days go by and Dallas did offer him a two-year contract.

CHAPTER 8

THE DALLAS COWBOYS

This was a dream come true for me as a dad. The funny thing was that even though I lived in Wisconsin and loved the Green Bay Packers as a child, my favorite team had always been the Dallas Cowboys. Roger Staubach was the quarterback when I was growing up. I can still remember going in my backyard at about eight or nine years old and throwing a football up in the air and running underneath it to catch my own pass, saying it was from Roger Staubach. It was "America's Team" back then, and was still known as America's Team when Nick was signed.

We knew this could be Nick's last shot at playing in the NFL, and he was going to have a very hard time making this team. They had some great players on defense and in his position as a defensive tackle. Nick was living back home in the duplex he bought, found a new trainer in the area and was preparing for the mini-camps and training camp. There is no doubt I was giving Nick some speeches about how important it was that he gave it his all and how he had to really work hard to make this team. I remember at some point before he left for training camp, I gave Nick one of my speeches.

Nick said to me, "Dad, I think I know what I am doing. I have been in this league now for a while. Have you played in the NFL? I think I know what I have to do, Dad."

This was another revelation for me because he was right, I was just being a dad, but he was at the point in his life he did not need these motivational speeches anymore. Nick knew what he had to do.

Right from the beginning of the practices, Nick was catching the eyes of the coaches, as we'd seen before. Nick was jelling with his teammates, and soon there were several players injured in his position. Nick literally went from last on the depth chart to practicing with the first string in no time at all. We could not believe it; it was a dream come true for all of us. Every day we talked to him, and things kept getting better. He was now practicing regularly in the starting lineup. Nick came home with a lot of practice under his belt and was going back for the preseason.

Again, he was practicing with the first string; we were waiting for the team to bring in other players to compete with him, and it was not happening. We had seen this throughout his career but something was different this time; they appeared to feel comfortable with Nick as their defensive tackle in the inside. I do know that Nick had bonded really well with his position coach, and he'd bonded well with Nick.

There were some very nice articles written about the coach, and Nick really respected him. How could you not when he was one of the most respected defensive line coaches in the NFL. We could not ask for a better coach for our son. That year Dallas had an extra preseason game because they were selected to play in the Hall of Fame game in Canton, Ohio, which is always the first preseason game for the NFL.

Nick was starting in this game, and there was no way we were going to miss it. This game was so neat. We saw so many of the past great players at the game; there are nice festivities and somehow Mary and I got down to the field right before the game to see Nick come out. We also met the Dallas photographer that day before the game, and he came up to us and asked if we were Nick's parents after we had said something to Nick. We said yes and he said, "I think Nick is going to be a special player for us this year." My wife, the ham she is, said, "Well, please take a lot of pictures of him for us, then. He said he would and he did. Right

WHAT A RIDE

Mary, Nick, and Bill after a Dallas away game outside the team bus

from the beginning, we felt that we belonged, not just Nick, but us as parents, too. We had not felt this in any other team in the NFL, and it was great. Almost like the great college days.

Well, Nick went out and had one hell of a game. There was no doubt he opened people's eyes that day. I cannot remember everything that he did, but he did have a great game. After the game we were down where the players come out, and there were many fans waiting for the players to sign autographs. Because we are parents, we do get to stay inside the gates to wait for Nick as the fans wait outside the gated area.

All of sudden, Tony Romo came out of the locker room. Tony was from Wisconsin, too, so I thought I would walk up to him and just let him know we were Nick's parents from Wisconsin. As I walked up to him, he began to sign autographs for the fans, so I wanted to be respectful and wait to say anything. All I know is that I continued to walk next to him for about two hundred feet without saying a word. I often wonder why he never looked at me or asked what I was doing walking next to him, and I always wondered if the fans thought I was his bodyguard because I was walking next to him.

The Dallas Cowboys

Then Mary yelled to me, I looked at her, and when I turned back around, Tony Romo was getting on the bus. I never got to tell him that day that I was Nick's dad. Just a funny moment for me, but it was amazing how many fans wanted his autograph and how gracious he was. The funniest part of this story was that as Nick came out of the locker room, we talked to him for a while and told him what a great game he had, and soon he had to leave to go to the bus. I would say maybe two fans wanted Nick's autograph as he walked to the bus. I guess Nick was not a known person, but he did have a fabulous game that day.

Nick remained the starter and at the next preseason game, which was in Dallas, Mary and I decided we were going. We wanted to see the Dallas stadium and even though Nick is doing well you never know if he will make the team. We did go to the game in Dallas. If I can say anything to anyone who reads this book, if you have never been to the Dallas stadium, I would highly recommend putting this on your bucket list. Go to a game in Dallas to be in that stadium.

I still remember walking into the stadium for the first time, and it was truly breathtaking. It is so beautiful and the excitement level is next to none. It has everything imaginable—and that is clear when you first walk in. I could not believe how big it was and how beautiful. Now when you get to see the field, all you say is *wow*. It is massive and the big screen goes from the 20-yard line to the 20-yard line. It is loud and there are many things going on before, during, and after every game. We could not believe our son was playing for the Dallas Cowboys.

Nick continued to do well every game and was really contributing to the team. He started every preseason game and even started the last game of the preseason. This was his fifth preseason game, and they were making him play a lot. It was a little concerning because most of the starters were not playing and you wonder why they are playing him in this game. We had seen so much happen to our son over the years that you learn not to count on anything. The game is over and the next day we wait to see if Nick gets that call of death, meaning did he make

WHAT A RIDE

it or not. The call never came, and Nick made the team. He had just come back from not playing an entire season and made it back to the NFL. Not only did Nick make it back, he was named the starting inside defensive tackle. This was the beginning of something special for our family. My son was now starting for the Dallas Cowboys.

Mary and I started planning which games to go to that year. We went to most home games and then looked at which games on the schedule were drivable, and we planned to go to those games, too. Nick was playing well, and the team as a whole was doing great. Nick and Milania were now married and rented a house in the Dallas area. We started coming in on Fridays and leaving on Mondays for the home games as we did when Nick was playing for Carolina. We were back into it, and all I can say is that it was better than great. We began to become part of the team, almost like college again. We started to know a lot of the players and coaches, and they knew who we were. The big reason for this was something that Dallas did that no other team Nick was on did. After every home game, the team would have a two-hour party after the game in the stadium. It was all you can eat and drink, and a lot of the players, coaches, and families would be there. Mary and I fit right in with this. The first time we went to the event we were there for about an hour and Mary and Milania left and went home. I stayed with Nick and we had a lot of fun that next hour. I was now meeting his football friends and they were meeting me for the first time. It was a party and we were taking advantage of it.

Well, the two hours were coming up and not knowing what to expect, I got another alcoholic drink. All of a sudden, out of nowhere, the security team came out and kind of escorted us out the room because the two hours were up and the party was over. Well, I just got this drink and did not want to let it go to waste, so I took it with me as I left the room. I was thinking I will drink it as we exit the stadium and then throw the cup in the trash. Therefore, Nick and I proceeded to the exit of the stadium and again, out nowhere, three security guards ran up to us. All I could think was: *I just got busted for taking this drink out of the room and I am going to be on the front page of the Dallas newspaper:* "Nick Hayden's dad gets arrested for taking a drink out of the party room." *Oh Boy! What have I done?* Suddenly, one of the security guards said into his radio, "I have a player, and I will escort him out." Wow, what a relief and what a new experience. *I'm with my son, and now he gets an escort to his car.* This was unbelievable.

However, it gets better. As we walked outside, two hours after the game was over, there are hundreds of fans waiting behind barriers for the players' autographs. I'd never seen anything like this before; it was amazing. So I am following Nick, he is signing autographs, and the security guard keeps moving us forward; otherwise we probably would have never moved on. The security guard took us right to Nick's car in the players' parking lot and made sure we got out safely.

I realize that I still have that drink with me and had carried it with me during this entire new experience. Well, I drank it up, glad I was not arrested, and we left for his house. I could not believe that I had just experienced something so awesome. What a ride home, and I was on cloud nine! Now we knew the routine after every game, and what fun we had each and every time.

There was another incident that year after a game. We'd walked out after the game and there was a party as usual, and Nick was signing autographs. I would always say to Nick that this person wanted one and that person wanted one, but the security guard does keep you moving, and I realize you cannot sign autographs for them all. Well in this instance, a little boy had a football and wanted Nick's autograph and Nick passed him. I yelled at Nick to come back, but he didn't hear me. The little boy said to me, "Can you sign my ball?" I figured, what the heck; the boy was asking me for my autograph. Therefore, I took the ball and signed my name, "Bill Hayden," with my college number, 71. The boy was so happy and I was, too. I just signed my first autograph. Later, I thought to myself, *The boy probably*

WHAT A RIDE

went home and his dad looked at the ball and said, "Who is Bill Hayden?" I didn't care. Hopefully, I made the boy's day, and it was my first autograph ever. I do have to say that, every once in a while after that, I did some more autographs after games.

Nick was playing really well, and Mary and I loved the entire football experience. It was mid-year, and Nick had started every game so far. You still worry about injuries and know that one injury at any time could end it all. We went to the home game at Dallas against the Minnesota Vikings. Nick was having a good game. The defense had Minnesota pinned deep near their end zone. Our seats were in the first lower section right by the end zone, and they were playing right by where we were seated.

The Minnesota quarterback goes back to pass. The quarterback is in the end zone, is hit by a Dallas defensive player, and drops the ball in the end zone. Everything was now in slow motion, and I see Nick start going toward the ball. It takes what seems to be forever, but Nick falls on the ball in the end zone and it is a touchdown for the Dallas Cowboys. I cannot believe it my son just recovered a fumble, which he had done many times in his career, but this one is for a touchdown. Mary and I are ecstatic in the stands and all we see is Nick get up with the ball run to the back of the end zone, looks at the fans, and begins to do a celebration dance. He is pretending to play a guitar (air guitar) and ends up acting as if he smashed it on the ground, then salutes to the fans, and runs back to the sidelines. We saw our son catch a touchdown pass in the high school All-American game, and now we just saw our son on defense make a touchdown. It was unbelievable, and all you could hear us say in the stands was: "That is our son. That is our son," repeatedly. We were very proud parents, and so proud of Nick. The amazing thing is, for the rest of that football season, Nick's touchdown celebration was a top ten touchdown celebration week after week in the NFL. I just learned something new; the players are practicing a dance so that when they do something big they can perform. No doubt, this was big for Nick.

The Dallas Cowboys

Nick, #96, warming up with teammates before a Dallas home game

Nick continued to play at a high level all season. This was by far his best season in the NFL and Dallas felt home to him and our second home as parents. That season Dallas was doing very well and it came down to the last game of the season to see if they would get a shot at going to the playoffs that year. They lost their last game of the regular season and did not make the playoffs. Nick started every game that year including all five preseason games to play twenty-one games. It was a very long season for Nick but a very rewarding season. At the end of the season, it was the first time we did not have to worry about Nick not coming back because he was now in the second year of his two-year contract. We were ecstatic. We saw our son get to the NFL, exceed by being a starter in the NFL, get cut by the team, get picked up by another team, get injured, spend a year out of football, get picked up again, start every game for Dallas, and now he didn't have to worry about another contract. As parents, we were very proud of Nick because he overcame so much and made it back to the top. What a ride.

For the first time in Nick's career, you could see he was being treated as a starter on the team. Nick went through mini-camps and the preseason started. There was something completely different now, he was a veteran and was a vocal leader on the team. He played very little in the preseason that year, staying healthy for the regular season. Mary and I said we were going to try to get to as many games as we could that year because Nick was always just one injury away from not playing ever again. The injury concern never leaves. We also began to learn that Nick was always injured in some way. Not enough to keep him from playing the game, but always some nagging injury. What we learned was that almost every starter has some nagging injury that they just have to play through. We felt something special about this year. Nick was a starter; the team had high goals and expectations. We felt part of the Dallas family. Because of Nick's wife, Milania, we started to learn a lot of the players' wives and girlfriends. We were sitting with them at the games. We now were in the club seats on the 50-yard line. The most awesome seats that you can imagine.

We had learned earlier in Nick's career that there were not a lot of parents who attended the games. Mostly wives, girlfriends, and young kids are the ones who attended the games, and Mary and I were the exception. We did not care. We wanted to take it all in, and we certainly did that year. We again had our routine and would leave on Friday and come home from Dallas on Monday. We were living the dream. We began to know the coaches more; we had friends and family that would come to the games with us. It was a blast. Nick's position coach that year had nicknames for all the players on defense. Nick was known as the "Golden Cock." The reason for this nickname was that he was "cocked" in the middle of the defensive line. The nickname stayed with him throughout his career with Dallas.

Mary got a great idea and made up signs that read NICK HAYDEN, THE GOLDEN COCK, and we took them to the games. Before the game we would go down below the stadium and they had a bar area were family and friends of the players could meet at and then see the players come through the tunnel.

For one game, Mary brought the signs, and when Nick's coach was coming out before the game, she asked him to autograph the sign. You could tell the coach was trying to get ready for the game, but he did autograph the sign and had a big smile on his face. Only my wife would have had the guts to do that and get away with asking a coach to autograph a sign right before a game. This was a special season. Dallas began to win, and they were on top of their division. The defense was playing real well as a unit. Nick was having another great year. We could see the confidence continue to grow in him. One of the things Nick was always known for was telling other players what to do, what gap to be in, when to shift, et cetera. This year was no exception, but you could tell he was doing it with more confidence. It was nice to watch him lead. He was becoming a staple on the defense, and we were enjoying every minute of it. This year, after the games, I started going out more with Nick's teammates after the games. I was having a lot of fun with them in the bars.

One night after the game, I met the left offensive tackle for Dallas. We started talking and joking with each other. I was also a left tackle through college and wrestled in high school. He did the same things but was an NFL player and clearly a lot younger and much bigger than me. We were goofing around and I ended up putting him in a single leg in the bar. He was hopping around and laughing. He was a gentleman and seemed to enjoy it. The next morning when I got up and asked Nick if he thought the player was all right with me putting him in the single leg last night, Nick said, "I do not know, Dad, but I will find out in practice today."

Nick came home from practice and walked in the door. Nick said immediately to me that the player loved it and had so much fun with me. It was amazing; we did develop a bond after that, and I truly enjoyed all my times with my son and his teammates while at Dallas.

The regular season was ending, and Dallas was on top of their division, going 12 and 4 that year and making the playoffs. It was such a big season, and they had a chance to go far in the playoffs with the hope of winning the Super Bowl.

The first game was at the Dallas stadium and was against the Detroit Lions. I talked about how wonderful the stadium was, but it even got better for a playoff game. It was so loud, and the energy in that stadium was unbelievable. The game went back and forth and was a nail biter. You are in the stands and all you want is for your son's team to win. In this case, it was even bigger; if Dallas wins, they play Green Bay in Green Bay, Wisconsin, our home state. The game came down to the wire and Dallas wins. It was crazy, the fans are going wild the noise level is at an all-time level that I experienced. My wife and I were jumping around in the stands saying, "We are going to Green Bay! This is going to be great." We were now going to the next round and still had a chance to go to the Super Bowl. We did have a victory party after the game and really were taking it all in.

Now Dallas was going to Green Bay. The entire week was so great. Nick, being a hometown person, was doing interviews on the radio and on the news. He was featured all week because he was from Wisconsin, played for the Wisconsin Badgers, and now was going to play on Lambeau Field. On one radio show, they asked Nick how this was going to be, and he said it was a dream come true. He was going to have so many family and friends at the game. And for a Green Bay Packer fan and, more

The Dallas Cowboys

important, a Brett Favre fan growing up, this was huge. Nick has always been an even keel type of person, but you could really tell how excited he was as he was interviewed. For us it was a great week. We called all family and friends and invited them to the game. We ended up having sixty to seventy people at our tailgate before the game. We got up there early and it was a gloomy day, but that did not stop us from tailgating before the game. We were having so much fun but the nerves started to set in as the game got closer. This did happen to me every game he played, and the nerves were like when I was playing football, but this time the nerves were even worse. I wanted to get in the stadium early to take it all in.

We did not get in as early as I wanted because there were so many people at the tailgate party, but we did get in early enough to see the team warm up before the game. Lambeau Field is another very special stadium to be in and we were Packer fans, but that day we were all for Dallas. It did make it hard because most of our family and friends were Green Bay Packer fans and were still hoping Green Bay won.

Mary would always say to family and friends, "I understand that you may not be a Dallas fan, but all I care about is that you root for Nick." She was always very persuasive with that and always stuck to her guns. All I kept saying all week was, "No matter what happens, this is truly our Super Bowl to have our son play the Green Bay Packers in their stadium."

Again, the atmosphere is next to none and you can feel the energy in the stadium. We had upper end zone seats, which may not be the best seats, but I can say there is not a bad seat in Lambeau. The game started and Dallas was winning. Dallas really dominated the first half of the game and continued to do so in the third quarter. Nick was playing well in front of so many family and friends and everyone watching on TV, too. It was a dream come true.

All of a sudden, during a play, an offensive lineman hits Nick in his knee from behind. It was a cheap shot by that player. Flags go flying from the referees. Nick gets up from the ground

What a Ride

and gets in the face of the player. Nick never touched him, but he had some words for what he'd just done. Now all the players on the field are gathered around, and another offensive lineman from Green Bay grabs Nick by the shoulder pads and throws him to the ground. Nick again gets up and gets in his face but never touched him, either, but had some words with him.

Finally, the referees break it all up, and Green Bay is charged with a personal foul because of the incident. This had never happened to Nick before, and it all was so fast. Here he is playing in his home state from the visiting team and all this is happening. I was so amazed that Nick kept his composure the entire time and never touched either of the players. That is great character to me and something I am extremely proud of to this day.

After that point, the game really got wild. Green Bay started to come back, but Dallas was still holding its own. It was late in the fourth quarter, and it looked like Dallas was going to win. I know from my own football experience that a game is never over until it is over, but I do have to admit Mary and I were in the stands looking at airline tickets for the next game, which was going to be in Seattle if Dallas won. How stupid. Green Bay scored quickly a couple of times and all of a sudden, they were winning late in the fourth quarter. Dallas had the ball and was driving down the field to their end zone. There was a pass from our quarterback to the receiver that became one of the most controversial calls in the NFL history. What we thought was a catch for Dallas down inside the 10-yard line got overturned and was ruled not a catch. The ball came back to the line of scrimmage, Dallas did not score, and the Green Bay Packers won. It was such a letdown, and Dallas was so close to going to the next level, but now the season was over.

We were in the stands not realizing what had just happened and we really became very depressed. We did have many fans around us that were so happy and celebrating because Green Bay just won. Mary and I just sat there as quiet as can be. We did come around pretty fast and just looked at each other realizing

The Dallas Cowboys

this was the biggest game our son had ever played in his career and we just took it all in. We watched Nick congratulate the players on the field and we did see the player that hit him in the knee come up to him and talk to him.

After the game, I asked Nick what that player had said to him. Nick said that he came up and apologized and said it was just in the heat of the moment. Nick said he was very sincere and it was just part of the game. Again, what a character statement for my son. All I can say is that this was truly our Super Bowl as a family, and the memories we will have forever. To have our son play in Lambeau during a playoff game was so incredible. That catch was talked about repeatedly for months, and finally it did come out in the media that it should have been ruled a catch, but unfortunately, during the game it was overturned.

One neat story from that game was a couple of years later, there was a football event in Madison that Nick attended. The player who pulled Nick down from the collar was at the event, too. They both talked about the incident, and we got a text on our family group thread of a picture of that player pulling Nick down by the collar of the suit he was now wearing for that event. It was hilarious. It does show that even after some tough competition, they can joke about an unfortunate incident that occurred, and the comradery of players is always something we saw during Nick's years in the NFL. To end this story, the other player who hit Nick in the leg that day was fined by the NFL for his actions.

This was by far the best year we'd had in the NFL. The team did well, Nick started all sixteen games again that year, and Mary and I went to fourteen live games, the most in one season.

The season was over, and again we had to wait to see if Dallas would re-sign Nick. Nick was a free agent again, but he did receive a one-year contract and a signing bonus with Dallas, and we were all very happy that he would continue his career with Dallas.

Nick came home with his family, and now we had a granddaughter. Nick took some extra time off because he did

WHAT A RIDE

Nick, #96, on the sidelines enjoying a big win against the Indianapolis Colts

get a small injury from when he was hit in the knee that had to heal. I now understand how important it is to do nothing for at least a month after you are done with the season. Nick had played two full years, and as parents, we could see the wear and tear on his body. He was twenty-eight years old and at times was acting like an old grandpa. That was so hard to watch.

We were so excited for the next season now because Dallas did so well the last season, and they were not losing any players. Nick was a veteran in the NFL and what a change it was for him not to always go out and prove himself. The mini-camps and training camps came, and during preseason Nick did not have to play very much, as most starters do not play to keep them fresh for the regular season. We decided not to go to any preseason games and wanted to go to as many regular season games as possible, knowing this was the last year of his contract. Mary and I would select the games we wanted to attend and always tried to go to all the home games at Dallas. We had our routine down for home games and took advantage of everything that the Dallas team offered to us. We had more family and friends attending the games this year, too. Nick also had many of his

The Dallas Cowboys

high school friends who came to the games. I enjoyed going out with all of them after the games, and we always had a lot of fun.

The season started and Dallas won the first two games of the season. They were starting right where they left off, and the season was looking good. Some key players were injured early in the season, and the team went into a slump and lost seven games in a row. The defense seemed to be on the field a lot, and it is hard to have such a good season one year to see this happen the next year. This is the NFL, and this is what happens.

Nick was having a good year stats wise, but the reason was that the defense was on the field more, so his personal stats were higher than usual. This is not always good, and the defense and offense were not getting good reviews week after week. Mary and I still enjoyed the games and would not have missed a thing, no matter what. We enjoyed every minute of it, but it was a lot easier to enjoy when the team was winning. That year Dallas went 4 and 12, just the opposite of the year before.

Nick had started every game for Dallas from the beginning, fifty consecutive games. That is very hard for any player to do and is especially hard for a defensive tackle. Nick was ingrained in the Dallas program and had proved he was a leader on the team. He was respected by his teammates and we had so many great memories and made so many great friends during the last three years. We really felt part of the entire Dallas organization and did not want to see it end. It became a waiting game, and we did not know what the team was going to do. We tried to stay optimistic. Nick's wife, Milania, was a wreck. She had made so many friends with the wives of the players, so it was hard to think that this could be the end.

Nick finally got his answer and it was not what we wanted to hear. Dallas decided not to give Nick another contract, and they were moving forward. This was so hard to hear. A parent doesn't ever want it to end, but we all know all good things do end. My heart went out to Nick. He had played his heart out for three years with a team he truly loved, and now it was all over. I can tell you that the emotions in the Hayden household the next

WHAT A RIDE

couple of weeks were very sad. All we had were the memories, and what great memories they were. The Dallas organization was a top-notch organization—the coaching staff, the players, and the owners all were great. We were all so blessed to be a part of what happened to my son, and all I can say is: what a ride.

CHAPTER 9

Another NFL Team, Or Time to Retire?

Here we go again. Nick had been through this several times. The difference now was that it was later in his career. Nick wanted to end his career in Dallas but still wanted to play football. Now it was a waiting game again. Does another team see something in Nick to sign him? Does Nick have the desire to continue to play? Is his body too beat up to continue to play? These are all questions that go through a parent's head, and you can imagine the questions going through Nick's head at that time.

It was hard to get information from Nick. You could tell he was disappointed that he was not going back to Dallas. However, Nick always carried a positive attitude and even though he was not hearing from any teams right away, he felt someone would call him. Well this did not happen for several months, and all of a sudden, right before the draft that year, Seattle called him to come in and work out. The excitement came back for all of us. Nick got on a plane to Seattle, and they work him out.

Nick came home and said the workout went really well. We were all hoping for that call that Seattle wanted to sign him. We did get a call from his agent, and he said that Seattle really liked him and they wanted to wait until after the draft to make a decision. We have been through many different scenarios before this, but this was a new one for us. Now the

WHAT A RIDE

draft meant something to us that year, and we watched it very closely. We knew that if Seattle drafted a defensive tackle that Nick probably was not going to be signed. Well, Seattle did pick up two defensive tackles in the draft, and we were confident Nick was not going to be signed. This is the hardest thing, but youth in the NFL can trump experience, and this is what just happened. Nick did get the news that Seattle went with their draft picks and would not sign him.

After the draft, we began to realize it may be over. We did not want it to be over. Again, it was hard to know what Nick was thinking, and he was very quiet and had the attitude that he had to see if anybody would come calling his name. The waiting game was always the hardest thing during his NFL years, and it is part of so many players' lives in the NFL. We had learned so many things as parents about the workings of the NFL that most people never know, but there are so many variables, and many we will never know, that go on with every team. We cannot forget this is a business, and I know Nick knew it the most, because he lived it day in and day out.

Time went by and Nick got a call from his agent during training camp to try out with the Cleveland Browns. One of Cleveland Browns' starting defensive tackles was injured during practice, and it was a season-ending injury. Nick again got on a plane and worked out for the team. He came home and within a day found out the Cleveland Browns wanted to sign him to a one-year contract. He got on a plane and he was now practicing with the team for their training camp.

The first thing we learned from Nick after his first day there was what number he got. Nick had had number 96 in college and was able to get that number back when he played for the Dallas Cowboys. That was his number, and like any player, he hoped to get it again. What we learned that night was that he did not get number 96, but he'd received number 71 at Cleveland. This is very interesting because that is usually an offensive lineman's number, but more interesting is that it was my college number when I played football. My son was going to be wearing my

Another NFL Team, Or Time to Retire?

number now in the NFL. I do not know if Nick was as excited as I was, but I was very excited. This was as big to me as my younger son, Alex, wearing number 71 in high school, but that made a little more sense because Alex was a left offensive tackle, as I was in both high school and college.

Anyway, we were as happy as a family that Nick's career was not over and we were going to be able to experience another year in the NFL. The funny thing is, Nick had to prove himself all over again. Nick does immediately start playing with the first string, but now has to play in the preseason games to get him back into condition as well as to continue to learn Cleveland's defensive system. Mary and I decided we were going to go to preseason games again because you never know if he will make the team, even though he is in the starting role.

One nice thing was that in the preseason, Cleveland played the Green Bay Packers in Lambeau. This game is a no-brainer for us—it was against the Packers, which was great. This game was the second preseason game. Nick started the first preseason game and did very well. He was fitting in to their scheme and I was enjoying watching number 71 on the field. We went to Lambeau Field, and Nick, as he had done every time he played against Green Bay, had a phenomenal game. Everything was looking good for Nick, and he was playing as good as he had in Dallas.

The following week we got a call from Nick and he told us he was injured. Nick said he injured his knee during the Green Bay Packers game and thought he could play through it, but in practice it just got worse. Soon Nick was not practicing, and there was no information on what would happen to him. After the next preseason game, we found out that Cleveland was going to settle with Nick and do a buyout of his contract. Nick accepted the buyout and now was out of football for a number of games, per the agreement. We knew now that Nick's football career was probably ending. Mary and I wanted Nick to play forever, but that is not realistic, not only for other teams to come calling but also for what Nick's body has gone through in his NFL career.

What a Ride

Nick after a Cleveland preseason game talking to family and friends

Well, the season ended, and Nick finally decided to retire. Nick believed that his best years in the NFL were at Dallas, and that was the team he wanted to remember the most in his career. The team Nick will cherish the most is the Dallas Cowboys. Nick did not play for Dallas anymore; however, it is the team he will cherish for the rest of his life. There are so many ironic things that occurred to our family, and there are two that really come out. First, as a child, Dallas was my favorite team, and to

ANOTHER NFL TEAM, OR TIME TO RETIRE?

have a son play on that team was a dream come true. Second, Nick, Alex, and I ended our football careers wearing number 71. For me, as a father, I could not ask for anything more. It is also ironic that if I had not written this book, I may have never put that together. What a ride.

CHAPTER 10

LIFE AFTER FOOTBALL

Mary and I have experienced something that most parents never get to experience, and that is having a son play in the NFL. We have no regrets, from the beginning to the end. We were able to watch almost all of our kids' activities through many years of their lives growing up. When you look at Nick's career, we never missed a peewee game or a high school game. In college, we missed one game because my younger son, Alex, was playing in a high school football playoff game and we decided to watch the Badger away game on TV in the afternoon and then go to Alex's game, which was in the evening. When you look at Nick's college games, there were thirteen games and a bowl game every year. We traveled to every game except that one we missed to watch my other son, Alex. We even went to Hawaii to see the Badgers play the University of Hawaii. It was truly an incredible ride through college.

I have had dads come up to me and say, "I think my son has a chance at getting a scholarship to play football in college, and how nice it must have been not to pay for your son's college." I always have to chuckle because I say to them, "Are you planning on going to every football game?" and the response is always yes. I say, "No matter where the game is in the United States?" and the response is yes. I then say, "Even to the Bowl games?" and the answer is always yes.

Life After Football

I then explain that there is a cost to all of that and not that I'm complaining about it, but I can say it cost us a lot of money for traveling, going to practices, bowl games, et cetera. Probably more money than it would have cost to just send him to college and pay for it. Then I would say, "If he gets the opportunity to play in the NFL, we are still paying for that scholarship with our son playing in the NFL." Every time I say that, the dad would say, "Well, I never thought about all that." I then say, "You had better start saving your money because there is a cost to that scholarship."

I can truly say that no matter what the cost has been, it was all worth it. Mary and I may have given up some other things for what we did, but we would never change anything for all the experiences we had throughout the years.

The NFL became another era because you never know how long it will last. We tried to go to as many games as possible. Mary and I averaged ten games a year during the years Nick was playing, and the one year when Dallas made it to the second round of the playoffs, we went to fourteen live games that year. In the end, Nick was credited for nine years in the NFL. For a young man, Nick really had to grow up fast, and he did.

Nick was never fined in the NFL. After his nine-year career, he'd still never received a fine in the NFL, and we are probably most proud of him for that character and how he carried himself through all the ups and downs throughout his career, even more proud than Nick being a starter in the NFL. We will be so proud of this stat more than any other Nick had in his career. Another neat ending to Nick's career is that I had an opportunity to call and thank Nick's agent and his financial advisor. Both individuals were incredible to work with and always had the best interests for my son. When I had talked to each of them, they had nothing but praise for my son for how he handled himself on and off the field.

Recall that, in an earlier chapter, we'd met with Nick's financial advisor. He'd said to me, "Wouldn't it be neat if Nick retired the same time you did?" and I basically laughed because

WHAT A RIDE

The entire Hayden Family enjoying a Florida vacation. From left to right: Emily, Alex, Sophia, Mary, Bill, Abbey, Layla, Milania, Teagan, and Nick

at the time we didn't even know if Nick would make a team. Well, I can say I am not laughing anymore, because Nick did retire from the NFL, two years before I officially retired from my job. It is amazing, but Nick did it.

    I can also say for all my children, we have been so blessed with all of their coaches. Never once did we have a coach that we had a major issue with. Every one of our children's coaches, no matter at what level of the sport, was a role model to our children. Every one of Nick's coaches helped him get to where he is today. In a society where we hear about bad coaches, we are blessed to never have had a bad coach. I look at my own career all the way through college and all of my coaches were great, too. One of the biggest mentors in my life is my high school coach. He taught me not only how to be a great football player, but also how to be a great person on and off the field. I believe

LIFE AFTER FOOTBALL

all my children have experienced that same thing. How blessed we are, and what a ride for all of us through our life.

Now that football was over, Nick and his family decided to come back home to Hartland, Wisconsin to live. Mary and I could not be happier, because we had not had Nick back at home for almost fifteen years, since high school. Nick and his wife, Milania, bought a beautiful house twelve minutes from us in the Hartland Arrowhead School District where Nick went to high school. Even though we had spent time at games and even weekends with Nick and Milania, this was going to be our time to reunite with them. We did just that. We now spend a lot of time with Nick and Milania and their two children, Layla and Teagan. One of the things Mary and I both wanted was to spend Sundays with our family. Nick and Milania did just that. Either we spend it at our house or their house, but it has become a tradition. We bought a pontoon boat together and we spend a lot of time on the boat as a family. My younger son, Alex, his wife Emily and their daughter Sophia recently moved back from Nashville after six years and now our families always spend a lot of time together. We love every minute of it, and having three grandchildren is the best. My daughter Abbey decided to move to Denver, Colorado, because she wanted to experience what both of her brothers did and be on her own. However, Abbey tells us all the time she will be coming back home someday. How blessed we are to have such wonderful children. We are enjoying life after football and we have the memories, and what great memories they are.

Once Nick retired, he went back to his high school at Hartland Arrowhead and asked if he could coach on the football team. Nick has been coaching for a couple years now as an honorary defensive line coach. Nick loves working with the kids and being back where it all started. Nick's head coach from Arrowhead retired but came back to Arrowhead as the linebackers' coach. Nick is now coaching with him and is really appreciating seeing him as a peer coach and developing the lifelong friendship, not only as a coach but also a friend. We

What a Ride

are also enjoying going back to where it all began, watching the Arrowhead football team play on Friday nights and watching our son coach. We do not have the parent relationships we had when our sons were playing, but football never gets old, especially at the high school level.

We still cheer on Dallas and spend a lot of Sundays watching both the Dallas Cowboys and the Green Bay Packers play. Nick does have an occasional Dallas party with friends and family, and we all still wear the Dallas gear. It still brings a tear of joy every time I put on Nick's Dallas Cowboys jersey that I was so proud to wear to the football games. We still know many of the players on the Dallas team, and it is so nice to watch them play and continue their success. We only have the memories, but what great memories and what a ride it has been.

The Ride Never Ends

I have always said that my experiences I learned in sports have helped me through my career more than anything I have learned in a book. It is about leadership, which encompasses things like teamwork, winning, losing, adversity, inspiring, praising, love, respect, believing in yourself and others, being on time, your work ethic, effort and energy, having the right attitude, passion, doing the extras, being coachable, being prepared, and my favorites—learn and teach, and live in the moment, and enjoy it all.

As parents, these are the things we tried to instill in our children, and this book is about a family's journey through life. It is about taking responsibility and being accountable for you first, and helping others through teamwork. We instilled in all of our children to be responsible and accountable. All of our children played multiple sports, went to school, and worked on the weekends. There just was not time to get in trouble. We held all of our children to high standards and to be respectful to others. One of the things Mary and I taught our children is to always do your best in anything you do. Live in the moment and enjoy what you do. If you do not enjoy what you are doing, find something else that you enjoy because life is just too short.

I've tried to show that in this book, and even though we had a child make it to the NFL, we had adversity with other things in

WHAT A RIDE

our life with some of the things Alex and Abbey went through in their sporting careers. However, Nick, too, went through a lot of adversity through his career and especially in the NFL, and it was never easy and many things happened over those nine years in the NFL.

Our children overcame adversity many times in their lives and learned to never give up. The one thing that Mary and I are the most proud of is that all of our children are very successful in whatever they do, and that comes from being a tight-knit family and always being there for them during the good times and the bad times. Mary and I are life learners and teachers. We now see our children doing so many of the things we taught them with their own families. We have been so blessed with so many things, and one of the things Mary and I learned through life is you must continue to move forward. We are very excited for the next chapter of our life with our family.

I would like to end with a quote that is near and dear to me.

"My father gave me the greatest gift anyone could give another person: He believed in me." —Jim Valvano

I hope that our children know we truly believed in them with everything they have done and that is why I wanted to write this book. All I can say is: what a ride it has been. And we look forward to the ride continuing in our lives.

ACKNOWLEDGMENTS

I owe a huge debt to my parents Bill and Charlotte Hayden for all they taught me growing up. Thank you for always believing in me and never saying no to the things I wanted to do or achieve. You both are a major inspiration in my life. I also want to thank my coaches and mentors I have had because all of you have made a big impact in my life by teaching me so much about the sports I played, but more importantly teaching me life lessons that I could use for the rest of my life after competitive sports were done. I also want to thank all of our family and friends who experienced the journey with us. We are so blessed to have so many great people in our lives and we have so many memories because of them. I want to thank my children for first putting up with their dad, but more importantly for what all of you have become in your own journey through life. I am extremely proud of my children.

I would like to thank Michael McConnell, my copy editor, for the countless number of corrections you had to make with the book. You were great to work with and I am grateful for all your work because English and grammar are not my strength. I also would like to thank Bryan Tomasovich for helping me get the entire book ready for publishing. The countless hours you put in to the cover, photos, and design are so greatly appreciated. Bryan taught me so much on the development of the book and was very fun to work with.

Lastly, I would like to thank Mary, my wife, for putting up with me through the book and listening to me talk about the book as it was being written and published. I truly love you, Mary.

ABOUT THE AUTHOR

Bill Hayden grew up in Muskego, Wisconsin, where he met his wife, Mary, in high school. He went on to college at the University of Wisconsin Whitewater and received a BS degree in sociology with an emphasis in criminology and political science. He also played left offensive tackle for four years for the Warhawks. Bill spent his first twelve years working in law enforcement, with most of that time as a detective. He went back to college while working and received a master's degree in criminal justice; he began teaching part-time for several years at two local colleges, Mount Scenario College and Concordia University.

During the first years in law enforcement, Bill worked second shift and Mary worked first shift. He was able to watch his children during the day and Mary watched them in the evening after work. Bill believes this helped create the family unity because both parents shared the responsibility with parenting. Bill left law enforcement to continue to have the right work/life balance when their children started school, working in operations, human resources, and financial planning through the rest of his career.

Today, Bill is giving back at the end of his career, teaching leadership to managers as well as mentoring and coaching executives. Bill and Mary plan to retire soon and spend even more quality time with their children and grandchildren and travel the United States and abroad.

www.ingramcontent.com/pod-product-compliance
Lightning Source LLC
Chambersburg PA
CBHW021409290426
44108CB00010B/459